The L.A. Teen Project

Ten neighborhoods, 42 kids,
and one microphone.

*What happens when a complete stranger
asks teenagers really nosey questions?*

ISBN-13:

978-1544896960

ISBN-10:

1544896964

For all the kids who gave their time, their trust and their voice
to this project,
THANK YOU

For Dylan's assistance with interviews, for her faith in me even
in the messy parts of any project, and for cupcakes,
THANK YOU

For Ted's incredible patience,
THANK YOU

If this book sparks new conversations,
among friends, parents, teachers, students and policy makers,
its mission is complete.

What is the LA Teen Project?

From 2008 through spring 2010, I interviewed forty-two kids, ranging in age from 13 to 19. I asked them personal questions about love, religion, money, gender, school, and family. This book is a direct transcription of many of those conversations.

With the assurance of anonymity, these kids spoke freely about their lives. And yes, there are drugs, sex and violence, but there are also deep friendships, family connections, academic and career aspirations and most of all, humor. Our teens are handling an amazing array of choices all day long, and I am pleased to say most are handling them with intelligence and grace. However, you may be surprised at the opinions and calculations that come into play.

I decided to create this book because I was tired of seeing only ugly or shocking reports of teens in standard media. I had been a substitute teacher in L.A. for a few years and I'm about to have a teen of my own. I knew the kids in my world were far more complex than they were being portrayed to the general public. I wanted to shine a light on their lives in hope that new conversations about the issues they actually face will be easier to approach.

These interviews all began with the same questions, but once they started talking, the interview subjects took the conversations into uncharted territory. My job was simply to follow, ask more questions and record. It was often a wild ride. As you read their words, know that most of these conversations were full of mischief and humor.

The words you are about to read are the exact words of the interview subjects with two very important exceptions: First, I removed much of the slang that would identify the subjects by ethnicity or economic class. However, I did not paraphrase or re-write their statements. Where any words are added for the sake of clarity, they are in parentheses. Second, I tried to weed out as much cussing as I could.

These kids swear like sailors. Most of these conversations were more swear words than standard language. The few cuss words left in felt essential to the interview subject's message.

These interviews took place in houses, parks, shopping malls, at parties, fast food restaurants, bus stops and on the street. The interview subjects are from Venice, Santa Monica, Culver City, South Central, East LA, Hollywood, Crenshaw, West LA, Boyle Heights and Korea Town.

As this book made the rounds with editors, I heard the same comment many times: "I want to know more about who said what. I can feel certain voices showing up through out the book and I want to connect their comments."

The decision to keep interviews whole or divide them into topics was difficult. Either format would have made excellent reading. Ultimately I chose to separate them into topics because I hope that each chapter can be used as a jumping off point for conversations about the diversity of opinions and experiences of that topic alone. This is also why you will see the same question asked many times. Each time it is asked, it is answered by a different person or group. Yes, three different people each describe scenes in which they were threatened with gun violence or even shot. Yes, several different people describe the process of making and selling kool-aid gummy worms. I believe there is information in the numbers.

I promised the interview subjects anonymity, which is the main reason they revealed as much as they did. But without names, I needed a way to identify each speaker. Each speaker is identified by a pair of letters. These letters are not their true initials. The same letters follow each speaker throughout the book.

There are a few very distinctive voices here. While conducting these interviews, the potential for radio or video was staggering. A few of the interview subjects were incredibly articulate and powerful speakers. Several were visually stunning. Some had such compelling stories that they alone could be the subject of books and movies. But many interesting stories and opinions came from quiet people. To gently coax a story from a shy kid hiding behind a mass of hair, to wait an eternity for a kid to find the words for an opinion he or she is still forming, these things can only happen in gentle environments.

I am also asked how I found and chose these interview subjects. I began with asking the people I knew, my friends' children and my daughter's friends. Then I hit the malls to hang out in the food courts until I mustered enough courage to approach a table with two or three kids drinking iced mochas or eating curly fries. I'd approach, introduce myself and ask if they'd like to participate in a book about teen-agers. Most looked at me as if I was a three-eyed monster. They'd shake their heads and turn away. This was hard rejection at first, but I got bolder and more confident, and eventually several great interviews happened at malls.

I made press packages for 20 different high schools across LA and hand delivered them to principals, asking them to allow me to come onto campus to interview students. Not a single one returned my call.

I also waited outside several schools and watched where the kids went. Many walked to fast food restaurants. I bought a lot of French fries for kids in 2010. One day I saw two girls sitting on a bench at a baseball game. They ended up talking with me for hours. Twice, I rode the city bus from Venice to Downtown after school and waited until some one engaged me in a conversation.

My biggest challenge was deciding when to stop interviewing. Truly representing the diversity of Los Angeles is impossible.

I did not get to interview any openly gay students. A few of the students I interviewed hinted and took me very close to revealing information about dating, but no one who is openly gay and dating felt comfortable talking about it. I asked for introductions, sent personal letters via adults who work with gay or transgender youth, but no one returned my invitation.

There are families from all over the world here. Teens from some groups were not willing to talk with me. I approached several students whom I assumed to be Muslim, based upon their clothing and complexion, but only one agreed to talk with me. I had a similar experience in an Armenian neighborhood. I know there is a deep well of information there that may be the basis for another book.

Still, I believe we did collect voices from an amazing array of people.

I recorded each interview so I could transcribe it accurately. While transcribing hours and hours of interviews, I could hear in every single one, the moment at which the interview subject decided to trust me. There is a definite change in the pitch of the voice. I can actually "hear" them relax. That's when the good stuff came out: the humor and the anger and the stories.

I hope you enjoy the interviews. And I hope they make you ask questions. I hope they spark conversations.

Shelly Blaisdell

**There are several TV shows
that are supposedly about the true lives of teenagers.
Are those shows anything like your lives?**

God no!
No!
Absolutely not.

BB, a 16-year-old girl
CM, a 17 year old girl and
NM, 17-year-old girl

Contents

Race, Ethnicity & Cultural Connections

Technically we're all African.

SL, a 14 year old girl

On some school forms and applications, you are asked to fill in a bubble identifying your race or ethnicity. What bubble do you fill in?

CM: I'm Caucasian.

NM: I fill in "other." I'm mixed with everything. I don't feel like I relate or fit into one category.

Are you ever offended by that question?

CM: Sometimes. I kind of feel like its no one's business. I don't see how your ethnicity and your test scores go together.

BB: I'm several variations of White, but I don't see why it's necessary to put that I'm White on a test. I mean, why? Do I get a higher or lower score on my college applications? Are they going to pick me or not pick me because I'm White? That's not fair.

NM: Yeah, putting a face or a name to an application takes away from your qualifications. A college application should be based on your test scores and your qualifications and how hard you worked in high school instead of "we need to fill this demographic."

CM is a 17 year old girl
NM is a 17 year old girl
BB is a 16 year old girl

What bubble do you fill in?

RD: I put Caucasian. I'm Caucasian and I'm Mexican, so I'm in the middle so I'm just, like, whatever.

SE: Oh, mine's hard. I put "other." I'm Chinese, Mexican, and Black so it gets confusing. I used to ask "Can I pick all these?" and they'd say, "No. You can only pick one." I can't be just one.

RD is 15 year old girl
SE is a 15 year old girl

What bubble do you fill in?

NI: As a joke once, I put Pacific Islander. I don't know why. Normally I do White. But every time this comes up I want to put "other," just because I think it shouldn't matter. And it always says, "This is not used to determine anything. It's just for statistical information." But . . .

I consider myself more as a person of the world than any specific race.

One of my favorite things we learned in my anthropology class is that nothing in nature differentiates by type. Animals, people, plants, nothing differs by type; they differ by degree. Most things aren't TOTALLY different. I think that's a brilliant way of looking at things, because then we see how similar everyone is in so many ways.

I consider myself a global person, but unfortunately in society, cultural lines are drawn and the color of my skin somehow, in some peoples' minds, dictates my personality, my sense of humor. It's the basis for a lot of not so great things in the world.

NI is a 19 year old guy

What bubble do you fill in?

GO: White or Caucasian. I don't know what the big deal about this is. For me it's no big deal. A lot of kids always say there should be more bubbles. One thing I often see on tests is where it says "White/Caucasian" and then in parentheses it will say "or Middle Eastern descent." That's kind of weird how they just lump those together. They're complete opposites. Not only do they look different but they are from totally different cultures.

I remember reading some story about some kid who had a huge epiphany about his culture when he was filling in one of those tests. I don't see the big deal about this. It's just numbers on certain statistics. I identify myself as White.

GO is an 18 year old guy

What Bubble do you fill in?

NZ: I am first generation Israeli in this country. My parents are Israeli but I don't feel like I am. But also, on those state tests, where they ask for my race, often the only option for me is "White." Look at me. Do I look White to you? It's just so messed up.

NZ is 17 year old girl

How many languages are spoken in your house?

AA: Two. Spanish and English. Spanish was my first language.

What language do you dream in?

AA: English mostly, but sometimes I dream in Spanish, depending on where I am and who I'm with. Like, if I'm dreaming of my grandma, most of it will be in Spanish. But if I'm dreaming about my friends it will be in English.

What bubble do you fill in?

AA: Oh I hate those. I wish they'd just put "human." Its kind of like, "Why do you care?"

Do you know why you're being asked that question?

AA: No.

If you had to identify yourself as Latina, Hispanic or Mexican, which would you choose?

AA: Well, Hispanic is the broad term. If you're Latina it's because you're a girl. So I'm a Hispanic Latina from Mexico. It also depends on where you are or what part of Los Angeles you're from. If I'm deep in LA, I'm Latina. But in Santa Monica, I'm Mexican.

AA is a 15 year old girl

Tell me about the word "Black."

CM: Did you see those girls who came to school last week? I've seen dark before, I mean really dark, but still somebody you could see when the lights go out, but those girls--

TR: Oh I know! I've never seen Black like that.

CM: They just came here from Nairobi. I swear, it's like they're purple.

TR: Are they sisters?

CM: I don't know but there's a bunch of them. I mean, I'm Black, but that's serious Black.

PA: I have a cousin who's orange.

TR: No way!

PA: Totally. Orange. My grandma still tries to say she's not one of us.

CM is a 16 year old girl
TR is a 17 year old girl
PA is a 17 year old girl

How much does your Armenian heritage influence you life?

NA: Everything about me is Armenian. I will marry an Armenian man in the Orthodox Church. That's already been decided.

NA is a 19 year old girl

What bubble do you fill in?

MH: Mr. F told us he always fills in "other" because he doesn't want to be classified. I've always filled in Caucasian, but I'm going to go with him and do "other" from now on.

SL: Me too.

Why?

MH: Because you're putting a label on someone, saying you're only Black or only White but if I put "other" I can say I'm from Sweden and Norway and all these other places. I'm not White.

SL: I'm Asian.

Really?

SL: Yes. A long, long time ago, my ancestors came from the continent of Asia.

JH: I'm Czechoslovakian.

MH: I'm Danish.

JH: My ancestors were Jewish, but my great grandmother decided to be Christian, so . . .

SL: There is no Jewish bubble.

MH: I know!

JH: I'm from France.

SL: I'm tan.

MH: Saying Black or White is just labeling my skin. It's not who I am.

JH is a 14 year old girl
SL is a 14 year old girl
MH is a 15 year old girl

What do you do in the Muslim Student Association meetings?

SP: We talk about our religion. There are different religions in there.

What bubble do you fill in?

SP: I fill out Asian, because they call us Asian as well.

Muslim is considered Asian?

SP: Sometimes. But not like ASIAN Asian. But Asian, yeah. I'm Muslim. Muslim is the name of a cultural group. My religion is Islam. And there are certain kinds of Muslims. There's Sunni, which I am, and there's Shia.   And there are a couple of more that I don't remember. The Muslim Association at school is a place where all the Muslims come together, but some of them are different. Some of them are Muslim but they're not Sunni or Shia.

At your school, do these groups get along?

SP: Yes, everyone gets along. And that's good.

Do you speak another language?

SP: Yes. My parents are from Pakistan, and their parents are from India, like before the split. So there's Gujarati, Urdu and English. I was born in Beverly Hills.

Does any one give you bad attitude at school because you're Muslim or Islamic?

SP: Oh no. But they often ask what I "am." Some people think I'm Arabic. My sister and I look really different [from one another] so some people call me Hispanic and some people call her Black.

SP is a 14 year old girl

24

What do you think about the word "White"?

HM: Everything we do is White if you think about it. Like the history books, it's all White people. Like all the history that we know, it's their history, you know? Christopher Columbus wasn't really a good guy. He didn't really discover America.

GA: It was the Indians. The Indians were already here.

MB: Yeah, and then he turned his back on them. And we celebrate that dude, but he's not really a good guy.

GA: We have a Black history month, but you don't see a Hispanic history month.

HM: I know, and the money too . . . Everyone needs money. It's kind of like worship. But if you look at the money it's all White people. If we had money with a Mexican dude on it, what would the White people think?

GA: They'd have a fit.

HM is a 19 year old guy
GA is a 17 year old girl
MB is an 18 year old girl

What bubble do you fill in?

HM: I don't see what that has to do with anything.

Why are you being asked for this information?

HM: They're trying to see what race is smarter. They want to see that the White people are smarter or the Asian people are smarter. They could do it to see if "These people need some help over here, so

Continued . . .

let's send some teachers over there." But they don't do that. They just do it to have statistics. But if they would do it to use the information in a positive way, to help people they see are not very well educated, that would be good. But I think they just do it for amusement.

Who is amused by this?

HM: The people who thought of doing this in the first place. Obviously the people who thought of this thought they were smarter.

HM is a 19 year old guy

When do you say "Black" and when do you say "African American"?

EA: I honestly don't care, but some people do, so I just say African American just so I don't offend anybody. Some people are really sensitive about it.

CA: I'm just like "OK, so we're Black . . . oh well."

RF: Oh it totally makes a difference to me. I am not this color. I use African American, but I'm actually White. I'm Italian, Barbasian and African American. When people say "You're Black" I say, "OK, but I'm also Barbasian and Italian, which is White."

CA: Sometimes I put "African American" but sometimes I put "other."

JC: I'm caramel. On those state tests I always look for "caramel," but its not there. So I choose African American. I am a few other things as well, but overall, I'm African.

What about those other things? Are they important to you?

JC: Not really. I don't really care.

Continued . . .

KG: I am African American, French and Japanese. When I look at the bubbles on the test I always think, "Man, there are so many types of Asian!"

KL: I'm Hispanic, and I'm Mexican. The first thing I hear when I hear Mexican, I hear "me." The first thing I think of when I hear Latino is "cholo." I don't like the word Latino. It makes me think of cholo and people think Mexicans are supposed to be like that.

RR: I'm a lot of stuff. I'm Cherokee, Mexican, Norwegian and African American. But a lot of people just call me Black because that's what they say I look like.

JC: You're caramel too!

RR: Yeah. But when they call me Black, they just leave all my other ethnicities out. And I don't think I should be put in that small a category. I am multiracial.

DA: I am Filipina and Irish and something else but I don't know how to pronounce it. It really bothers me that you're either one or the other and when they say "little White girl" it really pisses me off.

Who says "little White girl"?

DA: A lot of people. Or "little Asian girl." And I'm like, "Dude, I'm both." Then they go "Oh really?"

KG: I look unusual, so people ask me "So . . . are you . . . Black?" and I say, "Yes, and I'm also Asian and Indian and French." But they think I'm Black so they think I'm ghetto or something.

CA: Oh I hate that.

EA is a 14 year old guy
CA is a 15 year old girl
RF is a 15 year old girl
JC is a 16 year old guy
KL is a 15 year old guy
RR is a 15 year old girl
KG is a 14 year old girl
DA is a 14 year old girl

What bubble do you fill in?

CC: I put Asian.

ZR: I put Pacific Islander. I'm Filipino.

MM: I'm Hispanic and Asian, but I put Hispanic.

Why do you mark Hispanic?

MM: I look totally Asian but I was born in Mexico.

Why do you think you're asked this question?

ZR: I don't know.

MM: Maybe to see how multi-ethnic the school is?

CC is a 14 year old guy
ZR is a 14 year old guy
MM is a 15 year old girl

God, Religion and Prayers (or not)

I'm a Jew . . . Foo'!

SL, a 14-year-old girl

Are you a religious person?

MM: Yes, definitely.

PO: My family is, so . . . yes.

CC: I'm Christian.

ZR: I'm Muslim.

MM: I'm Catholic, and he's Buddhist.

HG: I'm like a mix.

Do you go to church?

CC: Yeah, I go to church sometimes.

ZR: I go to a Consulate, but not very often. But I do prayers. Before I pray, I have to wash my body.

CC is a 15 year old guy
ZR is a 14 year old guy
MM is a 15 year old girl
HG is a 14 year old girl

Do you believe in God?

SL: Yes! And I love how scientists are proving the days of creation . . . proving the little pieces of the bible together.

MH: Really, I mean, how else could apes evolve into humans? The scientific stuff works, but how did the apes get there in the first place? Yes, they evolved from little scum, but how did the scum get there?

SL is a 14 year old girl
MH is a 15 year old girl

Are you a religious person?

KL: Yeah.

What are your prayers like?

KL: Everything really, what ever I want at that time. What's wrong with my life at that time.

KL is a 15 year old guy

Are you a religious person?

KG: I wasn't raised in the church, but I was raised to abide by The Father. I know the Ten Commandments. I respect people and they respect me. I'll go to church. I'm Christian. I do believe in a maker. But some of my friends emphasize the religious thing that makes it all so unbelievable. One of my friends says you need to follow all these rules or you won't get into the gates of heaven. And it just makes me so mad, because it's like he believes I have to [do things his way], because he's this extremely holy person, and I just can't deal with that.

KG is a 14-year-old girl

Do you believe in God?

JC: I believe in what science can prove. I don't believe in god. I don't believe in 'Oh, believe in this guy and you'll go to heaven." In fact, I DO believe in heaven and hell, but not in god. If he is real, why doesn't he just talk to us right now?

In moments of crisis or sadness, is there a part of you that wants there to be an over seeing guide in all this or do you remain scientific?

JC: If you don't believe in god, you have to believe in yourself.

JC is a 15 year old guy

Are you a religious person?

PO: Yeah, I believe in God. When I was a little girl, my sister, she would always make me pray in the night. Even though sometimes I was so sleepy I didn't want to do it. I still do it to this day, even though sometimes I don't because I'm too tired. My parents wanted me to go to church every Sunday. But ever since I had my daughter I don't really go.

Will you raise your girl Catholic?

PO: I would prefer that she's Catholic, but I won't force it on her. I care, but that's her life. You know?

Are you a good mom?

PO: I don't know. You might think you're a good mom, but sometimes you might be too strict. Or you might be too laid back and that might not be what the child needs. I don't think you can be a perfect mom. I think I'm a pretty good mom. I'm not going to win the "Good Mom Award" but I'm there. And I'll teach her about God.

PO is an 18 year old girl

Have you ever had a deep experience of a religion other than your own?

SG: I went to India over the summer, and went to lots and lots of monasteries. And one day I wandered off and found this young guy sitting in a room by himself in this haze of incense. It was really intense. I sat with him for about 20 minutes and I suddenly realized that this is what he "does." And the idea of faith and the path that a lot of these monks take, it's been this way for thousands of years. They get up and they pray. They drink tea and pray, then eat and do chores and pray some more and go to bed and get up and do it all again . . . for years. There wasn't one day where you do this. This is everyday. Such an incredibly different way of living your life.

SG is an 18 year old guy

Are you a religious person?

AA: I'm Catholic. My parents are Catholic. After my grandma died, they kind of got more strong with it.

Have you ever felt God?

AA: Not really. It's more like someone to talk to in the middle of the night when you're bored.

What are those conversations in the night about?

AA: I'm not sure. They're "OK, this is what I did today." and "I wish I did this different." And praying for other people.

If you've never felt God, what keeps you believing?

AA: There are a lot of things that people believe in that they haven't felt. Like love. Its something you're hoping for.

Is it something YOU are hoping for?

AA: Yeah, I guess so.

Have you had your Confirmation?

AA: No. I'm not going to.

RA: Yes she is! (Her younger sister interjects from across the room.)

Why not?

AA: I don't know. I just don't want my confirmation to happen for some reason. I'd rather just stay where I am right now. I feel like if I have a confirmation then I'm . . . not trapped, but . . . you're really Catholic then. And what if I change my mind in the future because of some weird experience or something?

Continued . . .

Do you have a relationship with Mary?

AA: I have a picture of Her in our living room. Other than that I don't talk to Her very much. But there are other things in the catechism that I don't really believe in, like the whole gay marriage thing. I believe that they should be able to get married, but my religion tells me that it's against the bible.

How do you reconcile that?

AA: I don't know. My family sometimes believes that they shouldn't be able to get married. I just kind of stay out of the conversation.

Have you tried to have this conversation with your parents?

AA: No. I'll just get ignored or put down or something.

Do you have any gay friends?

AA: Yes, I have a few gay friends.

When they come to your house, how do your parents react?

AA: I don't think they even know that they are gay or lesbian.

Are they any gay people at church?

AA: Not that I know of.

Is it difficult to be Hispanic and gay?

AA: Oh, that's something that a lot of people don't like in my religion. If my great grandmother came to the United States and met a gay person who is Hispanic and Catholic she'd probably shun them. Our generation is probably a lot more welcoming than our parents' or grandparents' or aunts' generation.

AA is a 15 year old girl
RA is a 13 year old girl

Are you a religious person?

DA: I am SO religious. I am Catholic. Now that it's lent, I go to church twice every week. On Fridays I altar serve, I help the priest. I serve every single week, and I know a lot about it, and I love it. I'd rather be up on the altar and helping with the process than just sitting there.

Was this always going to be part of you or did your parents give this to you?

DA: My parents gave this to me. When I was little, I hated church. They would force us to go. I hated the homilies. I hated being tired. I hated everything about it. But now I love it.

CA: I have a friend whose parents are forcing her to be atheist.

What religion would she like to practice?

CA: She doesn't know, but she just knows she wants to believe in God but her parents won't let her.

DA is a 14 year old girl
CA is a 15 year old girl

Have you ever felt God?

NI: I dig the whole Gaia theory, that the earth is a living, breathing organism that has form and function and balance. Moments that I've had have always been in nature, where I feel, not necessarily the presence of a higher being, but more like the presence of . . . ALL things. I've had lots of moments like that.

NI is a 19 year old guy

God is . . . Everywhere.

A 17-year-old guy

Have you ever really felt God?

RD: I've been going to church ever since I was little, but I've never really felt His powers around me. But I have felt at times that I need Him. Like you see in movies when someone says "God, please help me." I remember asking God to help my grandpa get better in surgery. I asked, "God, can you please help my grandfather?" And four days later he felt fine. He had a beer.

When you were appealing to God, did you believe that He could hear you?

RD: I was hoping. I used to feel God was around me [when I was younger]. It felt good.

RD is a 15 year old girl

Have you ever felt God?

RR: I'm spiritual, but I'm not exactly religious. I believe in God, but I don't believe that you have to live by a bunch of rules.

Do you pray?

RR: Yeah. I thank God for being here, for the food that we have, stuff like that.

RR is a 15 year old girl

Have you ever felt God?

SE: I go to Bible camp every year. But I don't really go to church. Some times I go "ok . . . Is THAT you?" I'm scared of ghosts. I believe that they're real. So sometimes I pray to Him and HOPE that He's real.

SE is a 15 year old girl

Do you believe in God?

SG: I want to say god is dead. But that implies that he was alive at some time. I would say that god is, personally, non-existent. I had an existential epiphany early in my life where I realized there is no god, no deeper meaning, at least that I could ever obtain. And that epiphany has allowed me to live my life in a much more content way. The meaning of life for me is what ever I define it as.

The word "god" kind of ticks me off. I totally have a lot of respect for agnostics. I have serious issues with the Bible. I throw out the entire Bible and any kind of organized, structured religion. I think it's horrible; it poisons everything. I know a lot of people would disagree with me.

But it raises the ultimate philosophical question: Why is there something, why is there anything, when there could be nothing? That's my only curiosity about a higher something. That's it: I have a curiosity, but I don't have belief.

I grew up Jewish. I even had my Bar Mitzvah. I had some ideas about god and some ideas about Judaism, but now I look back on those moments and realize how naive it was. That education has been great because it gives me my base to argue against it.

SG is an 18-year-old guy

Do you ever feel like you have to educate people about your religion?

I had someone say to me "You don't look Jewish" and I said, "I can't say you don't look Christian."

SL is a 14 year old girl

Can you be Muslim and not practice Islam?

SP: Yeah, but if you don't pray at certain times, or if you do a really bad sin, you won't be considered Muslim. We pray everyday, five times a day. Our prayers are called.

What happens if its time for prayers and you're in the middle of math class?

SP: You can make it up.

Do you do all five prayers every day?

SP: Well, my mom reminds me. Like when I come home from school I've already missed one, but she says I can make up for it. There's one at one o'clock and one at three o'clock and one at five o'clock in the morning.

Do you get up for the five a.m. prayers?

SP: No! But my dad does.

What are your prayers like?

SP: It's like thank you for everything He's given us. For Muslims, the solution to every problem is prayer.

Do you tell the school that you need time for prayers?

SP: You can. My cousin gets off from school at twelve on Fridays, because Friday is the main day for prayers. But Monday through Thursday you can just make it up when you get home. I've been to Saudi Arabia for Hajj.

SP is a 14 year old girl

Have you ever felt God?

GA: Yes. Some guy pointed a strap [gun] at me.

What did he want?

GA: He was gang banging. It was some fool from Michigan. I just tripped out. I didn't know what to think. I don't know. I started thinking about God and stuff like that.

Do you think that experience opened you up to God who is always there, or did God see you in trouble and come to you, or was it something else?

GA: Yeah, I think He watches over me. Sometimes I feel like I have a guardian angel. I don't know why, but I do feel protected at times. I've been praying to St. Judas Tadeo a lot. I pray every day. I pray the same prayer everyday: to watch over my son and my baby's daddy and my family.

Also, when my son got diagnosed with bronchitis. They said he was going to die. That time I prayed a lot to God. That's why I know He's there, because He watched over my son.

My dad is Jehovah's Witness and my mom is Catholic. I chose Catholic. Father G baptized me when I was pregnant.

GA is a 17 year old girl

Have you ever felt God?

NM: No. But I think that maybe when family members have passed away I've felt . . . something. I don't know. I'm not sure if I'm agnostic. I was raised really religious. It was forced on me. When you're young, you believe what you're told to believe. I don't commit to one religion and I don't necessarily believe in a god, and I don't believe in organized religion. When people ask me about my religion I say, "I believe in being a good person."

NM is a 17 year old girl

Have you ever felt God?

BB: No. I don't believe in god. I've never seen anything. My family is really religious. I'm Jewish. My parents go to synagogue. They tried to force it on me my whole life. I even had a Bat Mitzvah. But it wasn't fun for me. I didn't get the experience that my parents hoped and wanted for me to get out of it.

I don't see why people think they should do all this good stuff to go to heaven. You should be doing good stuff anyway. We're just going to rot in the ground. We just die. Or maybe we're reincarnated, but I don't believe in heaven or hell. I don't believe in god.

Was that hard for your parents?

BB: Yeah. They were really mad at first. But now that I'm a bit older they realize that I feel this way now, and maybe it will change later, but they can't push it on me.

BB is a 16 year old girl

Do you and your friends talk about the concept of God?

GK: Not really. We're all pretty religious-less.

How about the concepts of honesty and morality?

GK: Not really.

GK is a 17 year old guy

Have you ever felt God?

CM: I don't think so. My parents went to church every Sunday and they were always pushing God. I went to Catholic school. I do believe in God. But I don't believe that you have to go to church every Sunday and I don't believe you have to recruit everyone to become Christians. I think you just have to be a generally good person. But I do believe in heaven and hell. And I believe in God and Jesus.

CM is a 17 year old girl

Have you ever felt God?

HM: I have. One time I was walking down the street and some fool pointed a gun at me. And I froze and I looked into the barrel. And he yelled "Where you from?" And then something pushed me to the side. And it was weird because I was already frozen, but something pushed me. And also one time I got shot in my leg, in my femur bone. I remember I was like "Please God, let me keep my leg. And I won't gang bang and I'll be good." I made a thousand promises. But I didn't keep those promises. But I did keep my leg. So I know there is a God.

Do you actively seek God, to have a relationship with Him?

HM: No. But I give thanks. I'm grateful for everything, to be alive. I used to be in jail, and I felt like I'd be stuck there forever, like I'd live there, like that was my home.   I'm grateful for being out, because I've been through all that. I've been to prison. After I got out of prison, I'm grateful for freedom. Even if I have nothing, I am grateful to be free.

HM is 19 year old guy

Have you ever felt God?

SL: One time, when I was four, I was really young, so I was just understanding the meaning of God. My grandfather had passed away when I was two and I'd never met him. I was sitting on the couch and I could feel my grandpa. And I was like "uuuumm . . . Hi!" and I could feel God just talking to me. I probably looked like a lunatic, but I could totally feel someone talking to me. I was four.

SL is a 14-year-old girl

Did you have a choice to go to Hebrew school or not?

SL: Nope. My mom was like "You're going!" And it just happened that I have such great teachers and this year I had my Bat Mitzvah. The temple is a part of me now. I've been doing it since I was in preschool. I'm going to be a teacher there and I'll be a counselor. I'm going to dedicate myself there because I just love my temple.

I love being Jewish. I'm so proud of being Jewish. Around here the prominent religion is Christian, or Catholic, or some form of Christianity. When I was little I wanted to join Christian because I felt like the loner out. So when I meet a Jewish person, I'm so happy, like "I'm Jewish TOO!"

It's so cool when I go to JCA, which is a Jewish camp, and there's like 200 people there and we're all Jewish. The first time I went there was in fourth grade and I said, "So, we're ALL Jewish?" It was hard for me to comprehend that here was this entire congregation of people like me.

I can't wait go to camp next year, its call NFTY (North American Federation of Temple Youth). It's a thousand teenage Jewish kids. I'm so excited to go. When I go, I feel whole. I don't feel alone.

SL is a 14-year-old girl

Are you a religious person?

NI: I don't necessarily believe in god as he is portrayed in Christianity. But I do believe that there are higher powers or energies or beings that are watching over the earth and the universe. I believe there is good energy and bad energy and they both play their parts. I believe in Karma. I believe there is some form of retribution for people who do wrong. I believe it's generally a healthy thing to do good for others and for yourself.

It's not necessarily that if you do something bad you're going to get struck by lightning, or that if you do something good that you're going to win a car. Rather, that the universe responds to your actions. Mean and ugly actions result in mean and ugly consequences and good and wholesome actions result in good and wholesome consequences.

NI is a 19-year-old guy

Do you like going to Catholic school?

KS: I think it's a good thing and I'm happy that I go to Catholic school. Because praying and learning about God . . . I just feel better. I think it's a good thing, a great thing, to learn about God and pray every day.

Have you ever had a day when you couldn't feel God?

KS: No. My dad is very strict about every Sunday we go to church and he's a Eucharistic minister and I was an altar server for four years. And my mom's a Eucharistic minister and my brother altar serves and we lector. So our family is definitely active in mass whenever we can.

KS is 15 year old girl

Do you believe in God?

SL: I believe God is real in terms of spiritually, but I don't think He's physically real. I believe He provides us the capability to perform wonders, but I don't think He physically does the wonders for us.

There are many different forms of Judaism. I'm liberal reformed. A lot of parents put pressure on their kid, if you're Jewish, to have a Bat Mitzvah, like you have to do it [at age 13]. But my mom didn't really do it when she was a child. But she got really happy when I did it and she got her Hebrew name at the same time I got mine.

MH: I'm not Catholic anymore.

JH: You're not?! What are you?

MH: I'm Methodist..

JH: What's that?

MH: It's what my grandparents are. I like it more because it's more of an open thing. Catholic is sort of closed in.

If your parents are Catholic, does that mean you are Catholic?

JH: I think so. Actually, I don't know what religion I am so I don't know what to believe.

MH: We did Confirmation together.

JH: Yeah, and then later, we went to her [they gesture to SL] Bat Mitzvah

MH: It all comes full circle!

SL: It's so freaking beautiful!

SL is a 14 year old girl
JH is a 14 year old girl
MH is a 15 year old girl

Are you a religious person?

MB: I'm Christian. That's just how I was raised. She [my baby] has a choice. I want to raise her to believe in God because He's good and everything. As long as she believes in God she can choose her own religion. When I was a kid, no matter how lonely I got, I would pray and it would make me feel better. I wouldn't do a routine prayer; I'd just have a conversation with God.

Have you ever felt His presence?

MB: Yeah, he's worked some miracles. Like when my brother died. My mom almost died too while he was being born. I've also had a guy point a gun at me. He was going to kill me but God has protected me this whole time.

If bad things happen, does that mean God is not protecting you?

MB: It's hard, because sometimes I say, "Why is this happening to me? I'm trying." But I think that it's just a test to see if you really have faith in Him. In the end, it's pretty much all better.

HM: I think sometimes people put themselves in bad situations. Like for myself, I have put myself in bad situations, like I'll go somewhere I'm not supposed to be, trying to do something I'm not supposed to do and something bad happens to me. I don't think God is responsible for that. You're responsible for your own actions.

MB is a 17 year old girl
HM is a 19 year old guy

Sex, Pregnancy and Parenthood

I'm really happy to be out of high school.
High school was an immensely fun
but also a very confusing time.
A very hormonal time.
I was just going crazy for a while there.

NI is a 19 year old guy

How many of your friends are pregnant or have kids?

CL: Lets see . . . one, two, three, and . . . oh four or five.

How do friends react to the news?

CL: Some get really . . . you know . . . like "I can't hang out with her anymore." But some get really close and friendships get stronger to help each other out. Like my friend had a kid in ninth grade and I help her. I baby sit and I hang out with her kid and it's really fun. I enjoy it.

GS: [A long time ago] when you'd think of a young girl pregnant, you'd automatically think she's a slut or something, but it's really that she had UNPROTECTED sex.   That's what people start to judge you on now.

Why are kids getting pregnant?

GS: Its pressure from the guys. They say "Oh, we don't need to do that [wear a condom]. You can trust me blah blah blah."   And girls . . . some are not that bright. Some are really vulnerable to what guys say.

CL: Yeah, some will fall for it. Guys do this thing called baby talk.

What is that?

CL: They go "Oh baby, you can trust me. Baby, don't worry, I got this. Baby, if you get pregnant I'm by your side. I'll own up." And its just talk to get in your pants and some girls believe it!

CL is a 16 year old girl
AR is a 17 year old girl
GS is a 17 year old girl

Have you ever required a guy to use a condom and he refused?

BB: No. Most of the guys I know are fine with it.

BB is a 17 year old girl

Is anyone in your school pregnant right now?

GK: There's a daycare center at my school. It's for teachers who have kids and students who have kids. Mostly students.

When we start one of our classes, the teacher always asks us "What's good?" And we go around the room and this kid says, "I'm going to be a daddy!" And we're all "NO WAY!"

Yeah, he got a girl pregnant and she's keeping it. And he's going to be part of the baby's life. Man, that is such a trip. And I'm SO thankful that's not ME!"

You guys all know about birth control . . .

GK: Yeah . . . it doesn't always work.

Why are teenagers getting pregnant?

GK: Alcohol. Its alcohol. Sure, kids are smart, but when you're really drunk and it's going down, its just like "what ever."

Even the girls?

GK: Yeah. Definitely . . . it's happened to me once.

GK is 17 year old guy

What is your opinion of girls who have children?

CL: Some girls made a bad decision when they were young and now they're living with that decision and it's not really a big thing.

AR: I get offended when people say young or teen mothers are sluts or whores. My mom had me when she was young and my mom's not a slut. She just made a bad decision when she was young, but now she works with lawyers and she's married and had two other kids and she has a great life.

CL: And I think it's cool when they take responsibility for their actions and take care of their kid and they make it better for themselves.

CL is a 16 year old girl
AR is a 17 year old girl

Are your friends committed to safe sex?

CM: Some people don't like them [condoms]. It just doesn't feel as good as with out one.

TR: And they trust the guy.

CM: Yeah but that's stupid, because you can still catch diseases.

Have you ever been in a situation where the person you were with was not willing to cooperate with your rules?

TR: No.

CM is a 16 year old girl
TR is a 17 year old girl

Are your friends committed to safe sex?

BB: I am the one among my friends who says, "You better have safe sex!" to everybody and I'm constantly asking, "Did you?" And they go "Nooooo." (She makes an embarrassed expression). Actually most of our friends do but some don't, and then I yell at them and they say "Next time I will!" And then they don't.

Why do they not?

BB: Because it feels better when you don't. And birth control is hard to get and condoms are not as good.

SB: Have you ever really had to stand up for your commitment to safe sex?

BB: I haven't, because most of the guys I know are cool with it.

BB is a 17 year old girl

What usually happens to the girls at school who have children?

GO: Usually these girls have to drop out of school. They have to work a couple of jobs to take care of the kid. Or they stay in school and that puts an extra burden on THEIR mother or grandmother. It's definitely a hard thing to do, especially at such a young age. Of course I'm sure there are wonderful teen mothers who do awesome things, but it's hard to break down the stereotypes simply because the reason stereotypes are so strong is because there's a little bit of truth to them, unfortunately.

It's really hard to be a teen mother, and it seems that it almost always ends up, maybe not in failure, but definitely in serious hardship.

GO is an 18 year old guy

Tell me about a pregnancy scare.

BB: I consider my brother one of my best friends. His girlfriend and him had a pregnancy scare. I have a card that gets me free stuff from Planned Parenthood, so I had to go get Plan B for him and give it to him and if he didn't have a sister to do that for him . . .

CM: He couldn't have done it.

BB: Yeah, and his girl friend is young. She's younger than me, so she wouldn't know.   So I was able to help him.   He was so appreciative.

What is Plan B?

BB: It's two pills and you can take it up to four or five days after you think you're pregnant and it just kind of flushes out your system.

CM: No, it's not after you think you're pregnant. It's after you have unprotected sex.

How did you get this card?

BB: When I was in ninth grade I got my first serious boy friend and my mom got it for me. My mom is really open about this stuff. My brother doesn't necessarily know that, so he came to me instead of to my mom. My mom is totally open about sexual stuff. It's the one thing that I can come to her for and know that she's going to be ok. My dad is not like that at all.

CM: A lot of our friends have had pregnancy scares. It's crazy how many have. I guess since it happens so often it makes it easy to talk about, to share experience and advice, like "You're probably not pregnant, and let's go get you a pregnancy test." No one's actually been pregnant yet. It's just a scare, but then you can laugh about it.

I remember [a friend] freaking out and going to Rite Aid [a drug store] with her and buying a pregnancy test. She took the test in the bathroom at Rite Aid and she said "It's not positive!" We were high five-ing and we were really happy.

CM is a 17 year old girl
BB is a 16 year old girl

There are people who believe that giving girls information about sex or access to birth control is saying to the girls "We give you permission to have sex." Does that seem true to you?

SL: No definitely not.

MH: No that's ridiculous.

JH: No.

MH is a 15 year old girl
SL is a 14 year old girl
JH is a 14 year old girl

What do you think of kids who have children in high school?

NI: I believe that one is not ready to have a child until they are much older and have had much more life experience. It's such a huge responsibility raising another human being. Kids in high school, they are consumed with such different ideas. They haven't yet figured out what they want to do with themselves. High school is a crazy time. You go out on the weekends and get messed up with your friends. You do crazy teenager stuff, injure yourself, get sick, I don't know. It's just an unstable time. It's probably one of the most unstable times in a person's life. So it's probably the worst time for someone to have a kid.

NI is a 19 year old guy

Tell me something nice about a family member.

GA: My son is five months old and he's my inspiration for everything.

Tell me about finding out you were pregnant.

GA: I actually took the test but I didn't look at it. My boyfriend saw it. So he found out before I did. I was too nervous to look at it. He said, "Oh crap!" and I said, "You're lying." So I looked at it and it was really light. So I went to the doctor. Then I told my mom.

How did she react?

GA: She was cool. What could she say?

Did your friends take care of you?

GA: I don't really have friends.

During all the hard work and emotion of being pregnant and giving birth and having an infant, who's looking out for you?

GA: I guess my boyfriend, my mom and my sister. And my two friends.

GA is a 17 year old girl

Have any of your friends have had a baby?

PA: My cousin had a baby when she was 16. And it's cool, because even though she's young, some people automatically think abortion, but she just learned how to take care of a kid. I love her baby. She's two now.

PA is a 17 year old girl

What do you think of kids who have children in high school?

GO: Obviously it's really, really stupid. I cannot explain how stupid it is for someone to get pregnant in high school. Yes, that may have been the standard a hundred years ago when the average life expectancy was 40, but there is so much time to live now. When you make that jump from being a kid to being a parent so early on in life, it's a decision you are going to be stuck with for the rest of your life. That's why I am so pro-choice. First of all, I just hate that word "pro-life" because it makes the other side, our side, look like "pro-death" or "anti-life." Bad choice of words.

Its taking away someone's rights based on [another person's] religious point of view. If you make them have that child, you are limiting them [the parent] and making them take that step into adulthood. You are forcing them into that life. How would you feel if you knew that you were a mistake? A lot of people want to have kids but just not early on in life. When they say that the time is not right, it's not right. If you make a mistake of not wearing a condom, you should be able to undo your mistake and get an abortion. I don't see the problem with that.

If you have the kid, you are ruining two lives: your life, your boyfriend's, and the kid's too. You are going to resent them and its one more generation of early teen pregnancy and maybe low social income and a leech on society.

At the same time, I am grateful for services at our school. We have a nursery, and there's Planned Parenthood with several locations in L.A. They don't push teen sexual activity but they know kids are going to do it no matter what so they provide the best care for you. It's great. Kids are going to do it no matter what. If you get pregnant, these places will take care of you.

GO is an 18 year old guy

Any girl has the right to have an abortion, but no girl should have the right to have seven abortions just because they are unprotected.

SL is a 14 year old girl

Are any of your friends pregnant?

HM: My girlfriend is pregnant right now.   We found out on Halloween. We took a test two days earlier, and it said she wasn't, but on Halloween I said, "Take the test again. I bet you're pregnant." Then later, I was kicking it with my friends, and I was all drunk, and she called me and she said she's pregnant. And I knew. I don't know how I knew, but I did.

Did you tell your family?

HM: Not really. To be honest, I don't really socialize with my family. They're not really my family.

Who is your family now?

HM: My girlfriend and her son, and the baby on the way. And my grandpa. I don't really have parents. Ever since I was little.

Where are they?

HM: I don't know.

HM is a 19 year old guy

Are any of your friends having sex?

SP: I know that some of them have done that. I went to a party with my [older] sister, and it was a high school party. The dad was home only, but he was downstairs in the basement. And the girl, she was in her parents' room with her boyfriend. Her friend was blocking the door so no one could go in. But all the big kids wanted to see and they pushed the door open. No one could see anything because the lights were off. But it was bad. It was really bad. We left after that.

Continued . . .

There's a certain kind of people who just think it [sex] is normal and there's a certain group, like me and my friends, where it's just like "No. My mom would kill me if she found out." So, it's just not going to happen.

When it is time to get birth control, will you go to your mom or your friends, or take care of it yourself?

SP: I will go to my mom, because she's the best person who can help with that stuff.

SP is a 14 year old girl

Is any one at your school pregnant?

MH: Well . . . there was that whole thing with [name withheld], but she's good.

SL: WAS she actually pregnant?

MH: Well, I know she and her boyfriend did it, but I think it [the pregnancy] was just a scare.

JH: Mr. G told us a story about these two eighth grade girls that got pregnant by the same twenty two year old guy.

Why was he telling you this?

JH: Oh, he's Mr. Random Talking Dude.

MH: My mom is really open. She wants me to be really informed about this stuff so I don't go around asking the wrong people. If I ask her anything she'll tell me. She'll always tell me what's going on.

SL: Yeah, my mom was the one who told me about sex. We have an entire book about it.

MH is a 15 year old girl
SL is a 14 year old girl
JH is a 14 year old girl

Have you ever had a friend really take care of you?

DG: Oh yeah. It's not a long story.   It's just when I was 14 or 15, I thought I was pregnant. I told my friend, and her boyfriend took us to buy a pregnancy test. We went and I took it at the McDonald's and I was crying because I found out I actually was pregnant. I remember I was telling her "Now YOU have to get pregnant TOO!" And she said "OK, but by who?" And she was going along with it, but I was just playing with her and it was making me laugh.

So you had a girl?

DG: Yeah. She's two and five months. She's a really happy baby. She's good.

Is her daddy around?

DG: Yeah. He's a good dad. Actually my dad has custody of my kids, because some stuff happened. So, I don't live with my kids.

Kids? You have more than one?

DG: Yeah, I have two now. I have a son. He's six months.

How did your friends react to your parenthood?

DG: They were surprised because before, I was always in the streets. So they thought I would just leave my daughter to somebody. But they were surprised because my daughter turned me good. While I was pregnant I couldn't be at parties, so I went to school and I got a job. I'm doing good.

Is your dad including you in the process of raising your kids?

DG: Not really. He's like, "I'm taking over." It's sad and a relief at the same time, because my dad is a good dad. But I wish I could be there. I want them to grow up how I want them to grow up. But with my dad, we can't tell him how we feel.

DG is a 17 year old girl

Tell me about delivering your baby.

PO: I had my daughter when I was 17. It was vacation while I was pregnant. On the first day back to school, I decided I didn't want to go, and then on the second day I stated getting contractions. But I didn't want to tell my mom. So I went to school and my friend said she'd take me to the hospital. So we jumped on the train to the hospital.

Why didn't you want to tell your mom?

PO: Well, she didn't know I was pregnant. You couldn't tell I was pregnant. I was seven months. I didn't want to tell my mom until you could see it, but it just never got to that point.

So I started having pains, so I called my friend, and she's already had her kids, so she said, "It's probably nothing." So I called another friend who said we should go to the hospital. So my mom took me to school. I'd usually go in but just go right out the other door. So I left my stuff in the locker and we [my friend and I] just left.

I had her at 1:30. My friend stayed with me. And my baby's daddy was there too. Then I called my mom and said "I'm OK. I'm at the hospital but I'm OK." She didn't get [the message] the first night so the second day I called again because I needed someone to come pick me up. So I called, but they didn't answer, so I called my sister and left her a message saying, "I'm in the hospital, but I'm OK. I just need someone to pick me up."

So later, my parents came to get me and they said, "We're here to pick up our daughter." And the nurse said "Oh good. She's fine and so is the baby." And they're like "WHAT!?"

They were mad. My mom asked what I had and I told her I had a girl and she said "Good! You had a girl. So whatever you've done to me she's going to do to you twice as bad!" I don't blame her. I didn't tell her.

My dad, he's really violent, but my mom calmed him down. At first he was talking trash about the baby, but now he's in love with her.

PO is a 19 year old girl

Boys, Girls and Gender

I'd love to be a guy. I'd be able to pee anywhere.
I could pee out the window if I wanted to.

CM is a 17 year old girl

Tell me about the word "Shorty."

GC: Mainly guys use it about girls.

AR: I think it mean the same as ho bag.

GC: Some guys use it instead of "girl friend." Like instead of "That's my girl friend" they say, "That's my shorty right there."

SB: If your boyfriend called you his shorty . . .

GC: Oh, I'd tell him to stop!

AR: I don't want to be called a shorty!

SB: Do girl friends call each other shorty?

AR: No!

CL: I call boys dogs and I call girls cats.

AR: I call my friends bitch.

CL is a 16 year old girl
AR is a 17 year old girl
GS is a 17 year old girl

Do you have guy friends?

KS: Yes, but my guy friends don't really understand girls. They don't understand periods. They think its just blood. They don't know the emotional stuff that's part of it. And they don't understand cramps, like how bad it hurts. They just say "Stop being so bitchy!" And I'm like "Well, how would YOU be if you were me?"

KS is a 15 year old girl

Are any of your friends gay?

BB: One of my best friends is bi[sexual] and another of our friends is a lesbian and they were together for a really long time and we had to put up with all their fights, and it was just the same thing as if a guy and a girl were together.

CM: No it's SO much worse when its two girls.

BB: Yeah, but they fought exactly the same way I've seen my friends fight with their boyfriends.

CM: It's only recently that there are so many gay people at school. And there are those people who, it's like, "You're gay. Everyone knows you're gay. Why won't you just come out yet? . . . and it sucks because you're so cute and somebody might want to hook up with you . . . but you're GAY!" I don't want to be that person who goes out with a person and then after they break up with you they say "Oh yeah, I'm gay."

BB: Well, sadly, I've had a thing with a guy and he hooked up with a guy during the time that we had our thing, and I was like "Oh. My. God." He said he was just drunk.

CM: Yeah, and talk about the other one.

This happened twice?

BB: Yeah. Kind of. But I knew. I don't see a problem with dating a bi[sexual] guy.

CM: But he wasn't bi. He was just gay. It was obvious.

BB: I know, but he was just so attractive . . . it's hard for me.

CM: No matter how attractive he was, his personality was just so gay.

BB: I know! Well, one of them I was just super attracted to but one of them I had strong feelings for.

BB is a 16 year old girl
CM is a 17 year old girl

68

Would your life be easier if you were a guy?

NZ: Even though everyone's equal now, it still does seem like guys have more opportunities than girls do and life is easier for guys than for girls.

Opportunities for what?

NZ: Well, I know that there ARE women firefighters and women police officers, but most of the time there's not. And I'm sure there's some kind of sexism in the army. I'm sure that in some situations women are not considered an equal member of the team because they are thought of as weaker or not as strong even though some women are way stronger than some men.

NZ is a 17 year old girl

How would you define the words masculine and feminine?

GO: I think of my grandfather. He was a mountain man. He was a horrible father, but he was just this badass mountain man. He was a hunter. He was like primitive man; he'd go and stay out in the wilderness for months as a time.

And Feminine is . . . it's . . . I don't know. Feminine is . . . voluptuous . . . It's sensual . . . It's mysterious . . . It's . . . aahhh . . . I don't know! I'm not good with women! This is why!

GO is an 18 year old guy

Do you like being a guy?

TB: Sure. I'm a guy. Some of my best friends are guys. We do guy-ish things.

Describe "guy-ish things."

TB: Well, guy things -- there's usually less thought put into them. More of "That looks fun!" and less of "Now, can I get hurt doing this?" And often times you do get hurt, but often times that leads to wonderful, hysterical, bonding experiences.

TB is a 17 year old guy

Is any one at your school Transgendered?

BB: There's this guy at school who is . . . I guess he's a transvestite. He wants to be a girl. He wears make up and wears his hair like a girl. He's really big and he wears tight girl clothes. He used to walk into the girls' bathroom and everyone would be "Oh my god."

CM: He used to hit on a bunch of guys and they'd be like "EEEWEE! NOT OK!"

Does he get bullied at school?

CM: Yeah. But he's huge. And if any one bullies him he beats the crap out of them.

CM is a17 year old girl
BB is a 16 year old girl

Is any one at your school Transgendered?

SL: A girl at my school went out with another girl, but the girl didn't know she was a girl. She used to be so girly.

MH: I know! She used to be so pretty!

JH: Her hair was so nice. I loved it.

SL: In middle school she started to wear boy's clothes. And then she got a boy's [hair] cut. She used to like boys too. But in middle school she finally went out with a girl, but the girl didn't know, because she looked that much like a guy.

MH: None of the guys knew it either. She had the voice too!

What about the girl she went out with? What happened when she found out?

SL: Oh, she was freaking out!

SL is a 14 year old girl
MH is a 15 year old girl

What are the attitudes at school about gay students?

BB: A lot of the guys at school are totally for girl on girl action, but if a guy even looks at them, if they even THINK he's attracted to him they'd go "Ewe! That's really nasty!"

CM: And then, just to make clear that they're not gay they say "No homo" after everything they say to each other, like "Hey I like your shirt. No homo."

BB: Yeah, "No Homo! No Homo!"

BB is a 16 year old girl
CM is a 17 year old girl

Are any of your friends gay?

RD: Yes.

Are they well integrated with the rest of your friends, or do they seem separate?

RD: They'll be friends with any one, but if you're the type of person who doesn't like gays, then they'll back off. Some people are mean to them and say, "Oh stay away from them, they're creepy, they're gay." There's also this thing where people call anything that's weird or stupid "gay." And that just makes me so mad. I'm like, "Shut up. I'm going to smack you if you say that again." I got one of my friends to stop saying it, but he slips sometimes and then he says "I don't mean it like that." And I say, "But if there's a gay person around how do you think that makes them feel?"

SE: I'm bi[sexual] so I know how it feels [to be teased]. It's so messed up. Some people say things like "Oh, there's the weird dude with the pink shirt. He's gay." or "There's the girl with the shaved head. She's a lesbian." You don't know that. Maybe it's just their style.

RD is a 15 year old girl
SE is a 15 year old girl

Do you feel pressure to be dating if you are not ready?

SL: Well, a girl on my team asked another girl to give her a hickey so she could say that a boy gave it to her. And the other girl said "Ewe! Why would I give you one?" They're both girls.

SL is a 14 year old girl

Tell me about the girls at school.

GK: Girls sicken me with the way they conduct their friendships. It's not anything real. They find these petty little things that they have in common, like the way they do their hair or what music they listen to or what they wear, and they think that they'll automatically get along based on that. They talk about nothing. Girls can talk for hours and not say one meaningful word to each other.

Girls cycle through friends. A girl can have a BFF [best friend forever] and then, a couple of months later not talk to them, like "oh, THAT bitch? I am NOT talking to her." They go from one extreme to the other. It's ridiculous.

Do you have any women friends?

GK: Oh yes. I have some women friends who I absolutely love and adore. The girls that are friends with me are not like that. They're true friends, because instead of building up to a big catfight we solve our problems.

GH is a 17 year old guy

Do you think the boys understand girls at this age?

JH: No.

SL: They're just like "Oh my god! They have boobies!"

JH: It's true! All the time!

SL: Sometimes I just want to say, "Honey, sit down. Let's talk. You don't understand . . . anything."

SL is a14 year old girl
JH is a 15 year old girl

How would you define the words masculine and feminine?

GO: I don't know. That's such a weird question.

Does your gender affect the other elements of your life?

GO: Totally. I love being a guy. Obviously whatever gender you are, you feel like you are the superior gender. I know I do. A lot of my time is spent chasing after the opposite sex. I'm sure that's how a lot of people's time is spent. I try not to get caught up too much in it. It's trivial and there are so many other things in life, but how that differs being a male compared to being a female... I don't know.

Yes, gender plays in our favor. When a guy hooks up with a bunch of people, it's considered manly, being a player. But if you're a girl and you hook up with a lot of guys, you're slutty. That's good. It kind of keeps the girls clean for us guys when we make our rounds. It's a horrible social standard but that's just how it is and it works to our advantage. So I'm not complaining.

GO is an 18 year old guy

What is the general attitude at school about gay students?

SP: A few years ago, my sister and everyone at her school were wearing yellow ribbons and I asked her what it was about and she said it was for a boy at her school who got killed for being bisexual. They have news [about gay students] in the school newspaper. I think it's interesting to read about it. When we first came to high school they showed us a list of all the clubs at school, like the Christian clubs, and the Muslim club and the Government club, and the Eco club and the Gay and Lesbian club. And they ALL said we can come join them.

SP is a 14 year old girl

Is it harder to be a man or a woman?

HM: I think it must be harder to be a woman, because you guys have to give birth. I'm serious. Plus, I think it's harder to defend themselves because the man is stronger.

DG: But in some ways I think girls are stronger than guys. Girls can take more pain than guys can.

MB: My mom and my tia and my grandma, they always tell me that the women really run the house even though the men think they run everything.

HM: Girls are way more jealous than guys. Guys don't trip like that.

DG: No. Guys are way worse than girls!

HM: No. Girls get jealous over stupid stuff, like "Oh she has nicer hair than me."

DG: That's stupid!

MB: I have way more guy friends than girls. Girls are too much drama.

DG: Yeah, guys are way more fun to kick it with.

HM is a 19 year old guy
DG is a 17 year old girl
MB is an 18 year old girl

Is it easier to be a girl or a guy?

KS: I like being a girl, but I think it's easier for guys. They can go anywhere they want and their parents don't really worry as much.

KS is a 15 year old girl

Do you have any friends who are gay?

KG: Yes. They're not openly gay, but I think they should be. The only reason they're not is because people would make fun of them. I don't think people should make fun of them for it. It's not their fault. But people would make fun of them, and they'd have a horrible time at school.

KG is 14 year old girl

Tell me about the words masculine and feminine.

NI: I think they both play a part in the universe and they both need each other to exist. Our culture and media lead every one to believe that you should be engaged in certain activities or attitudes based upon your gender. But I don't believe that's essential to my representing my gender.

NI is a 19 year old guy

How would you define the words masculine and feminine?

MH: I would consider myself feminine.

SL: What do you mean by that? Like a cat? Meow?

JH: No, that's feline!

SL: Oooooooh . . .

MH is a 15 year old girl
SL is a 14 year old girl
JH is a 14 year old girl

Are any of your friends gay?

MB: Yeah. I got respect for them. Sometimes I have more fun with them than with other friends.

HM: Gay girls or dudes?

MB: Dudes. I'll kick it with gay girls too, as long as they've got respect.

Is it difficult to be Hispanic and gay?

MB: I've got two family members who are gay, one girl and one guy, and it's ok. I don't see any difference really except how they feel, but that's them.

HM: I don't have any gay family, but I think gay girls are fun.

GA: Shut up!

HM: I'm serious. I think their personalities are better, because they're girls, which is nice, but they think . . .

GA: Like a guy?

HM: Yeah.

GA: OK, but there's tomboys too, like me. I was raised by all men and they treat me like a guy but I'm not gay.

HM: True. But I'm just saying . . .

HM is a 19 year old guy
MB is an 18 year old girl
GA is a 17 year old girl

Are any of your friends gay?

HG: Yes.

ZR: Sure.

Is school a difficult place for them or not?

HG: Not really. They only admit it to a few people. Like us.

ZR: My best friend, you couldn't tell he's gay until he tells you. But once he tells you then you start to notice, and then you'll get those awkward moments. It's funny.

HG: He said he likes guys because they don't complain as much.

ZR: He says that if you like someone you should just like them not based on what gender they are.

HG: Yeah, so I guess he's not gay, he's like bi[sexual].

HG is a 14 year old girl
ZR is a 14 year old guy

Do you talk to your parents about your crushes?

RF: I can't talk to my mom about boys at all. She doesn't want me to have boyfriend. So what am I supposed to do, love a girl or something?

Would she be OK with that?

RF: Either way she'd be mad. And I don't want that option.

RF is a 15 year old girl

Tell me about being in love.

NI: Love is when a man and woman, or a man and a man, or a woman and a woman, find each other and they realize that are made for each other and they just want to be together all the time. And that's a beautiful thing.

NI is a 19 year old guy

Are you dating?

AA: Yes. It's really complicated.

In what way?

AA: There's a lot of drama. Depending on who you're dating and what baggage they come with. It's complicated, but you don't really want it to be simple either though, because then it's no fun. It's hard to explain.

Have you been seeing one person for a while?

AA: We went out the whole summer, then we broke it off, and we just started seeing each other again.

Do the guys have the same take on dating that the girls do?

AA: A lot of the guys right now . . . their libido really drives their instincts right now. But it really depends on what kind of guy it is.

AA is a 15 year old girl

Are you dating?

SP: No. I asked my mom when can I start dating and she said, "When you're married."

SP is a 14 year old girl

Fighting

My dumb ass friends
decided to fight each other in the back yard,
just for fun.

SG is an 18 year old guy

Have you ever been in a fight?

SE: Well, I got in a not-so-serious fight recently. You know how people "go body"?

No. What does that mean?

SE: It's just kind of like fake fighting, like wrestling, but not to really hurt them. Well this girl and I, we went body and I accidentally hurt her. I kind of choked her.

If it's not supposed to hurt, then what is it for?

SE: It's kind of for fun, like if you're bored. It's like "I want to hurt you but I'm laughing at the same time."

Who goes body? Enemies or friends?

SE: Friends, but sometimes enemies. If they don't want to get caught by teachers, they'll go body to make it look like a game, to make it not look like real physical violence. Security comes around a lot and if you get caught really fighting you'll get suspended.

Have you ever been suspended?

SE: No, not yet.

You say that like its inevitable.

SE: Yeah, maybe.

SE is a 15 year old girl

What is "going body?" Is it a fight?

CM: Yeah, everything is open to hit except your face. You "agree" to go body. Mostly guys do it, not many girls do it. I guess ghetto girls do.

Is it playful or is it angry?

CM: It depends. Guys will say, "I'm bored. Let's go body." They do it for practice in case they get in a real fight. But it can go from friendly to a real fight to brutal easily.

CM is a 17 year old girl

Have any of your friends joined a gang?

MB: I've seen so many of my friends get sucked into that scene. It's so frustrating, especially when you see the people you love, that you've known your whole life, who will look you in the eyes and just completely deny any possibility of connection. Then they are like "I've got your back, but while your back is turned, I might take your wallet." It's just how these people interact, its constant lying, constant stealing.

GK: What do you mean "these people"? You're not being racist are you?

MB: No. It falls into any category. You're talking about a lifestyle, or a desired lifestyle. I wouldn't even call it a gangster lifestyle. I'd call it a hood lifestyle. It's all about putting it down for [your neighborhood]. It's not just gangs. Gangs are a part of it, but it's just people.

MB is a 17 year old guy
GK is a 17 year old guy

Have you ever been in a fight?

GO: I was at camp, a sleep away camp in San Francisco. I was going into eighth grade and these two guys made fun of me for being Jewish and I proceeded to fight them. And my other friend joined me, so it was kind of two on two and everyone got really hurt. I would like to think I won, but it got broken up eventually. They actually let me off the hook just because there were a lot of Jews in camp.

GO is an 18 year old guy

Do girls bully more than boys do?

JH: I think it's a completely different kind of bullying. It's not like in the movies. Not at all.

MH: No. It's not like you see in movies where someone says, "Hey punk!" and shoves them in a locker. It's not like that at all.

Then what is it?

JH: Excluding other girls, or making fun of them.

SL: I get made fun of all the time.

Why?

SL: Me? Oh, I'm so easy to make fun of. I'm an awkward, weird girl.

JH is a 14 year old girl
MH is a 15 year old girl
SL is a 14 year old girl

Have you ever been in a fight?

TB: I've never instigated a fight. At my school, fighting is a daily thing. They have their own campus police force. They handle two or three fights a day, from small to big. Most of the time they say it's gang related. In truth they WANTED it to be gang related. In many cases, yes they [gangs] are involved, but not always.

There's also the fad of tagging or writing your name on things. And the random slashing of somebody, which is just an excuse to create conflict, to put some sort of substance in your life. So everyday there is menial stupid stuff going down. Fights start just by people looking at each other wrong. I mean, hold eye contact with someone too long and there's immediately suspicion and then aggression.

Someone challenged me to a fight. I was extremely aggravated with the situation so I agreed. Then school got out and I was crossing the bridge and the kid walked up next to me and said "Alright, let's go do this." And he was smiling. And I knew if he was fighting me he wouldn't be smiling, so I asked, "This fight is between just me and you, correct?" and he just said, "We'll see. We'll see what's up." So I knew something was wrong. We started going down the stairs. I heard someone approach and immediately felt something make contact—a full blow to the back of my head.

Luckily I wasn't knocked unconscious. I turned around and it was a kid I'd seen in a few of my classes. I forget his name. It's not very important. He said, "That's how it's done in the [name withheld] gang, Homie."

I kind of giggled at that point. And I looked back at this kid who wanted to fight me. I was situated in between these two guys in the stairwell, and this kind of thing is so normal that people just pass you. It's just flocks of students coming down the stairs. They just stay a few feet away. So this kid looked back at me, like he was almost questioning it, especially because I didn't try to fight back, which is exactly what they wanted, to give them just cause to jump me.

So I said "Do you still want to fight me?" And he said yes, so we walked out toward the bike racks and I saw a group of kids, and I

Continued . . .

knew they were the gang that this kid was affiliated with. So we walked up to the group. And I knew a few of the guys. One of the guys I take weight training with, he quietly said to me, "Man, don't do this. You know what's going to happen."

And I said "Well, this guy challenged me to a fight." And he said "I know. I know he's bitch, but it's family. I can't . . . " He's a very polite guy. That was only the second time I'd ever heard him speak. He was my weight-training partner pretty much every day. A very stoic kind of guy.

It was all ego, I know. He [the first kid] didn't want to fight me, that scene just proved it. That changed my perspective on a lot of things. I've seen so many people try to instigate fights. I think sometimes it's not even about aggression against the other person, its almost like its just something to do. It's excitement for them.

TB is a 17 year old guy

Have you ever been in a fight?

SG: I've seen a few street brawls. And it always seems ridiculous to me. They start over something ridiculous. And it's a disturbing thing to watch. I trained in jujitsu and did a couple of competitions and got my ass handed to me every time. I realized that part of the problem was that I'd never met this person and I had no ill will toward them, but my object was to hurt them until they gave up.

It's such an angry, aggressive thing, especially street fights. You wish it could be a different way. They're brutal sometimes. I saw a fight on the Promenade (an open air shopping area). And I don't even know what this fight was about, but one of the kids, who wasn't even in the fight, he was just a bystander, it wasn't even his deal, but he came in with a skateboard and just cracked a kid's head open with it. He just came out of nowhere. I saw this. And the ambulance came and there was a huge commotion. And I wonder what he was thinking at that time. He could have killed him, you know?

SG is an 18 year old guy

Have you ever been in a fight?

MH: No, but we see them at school. I think it's awful. I don't think they should fight. I mean we're all in the same school. We're supposed to be learning. This is supposed to be [preparing us] for our future. So what do you want in your future? Fighting? I mean, what is your problem?

There was one fight recently. Some girl said another girl nudged her in the hallway. And she said, "What is your problem?" And she said, "It was an accident." And then it turned into this whole thing. And she said she'd meet her after school and it turned into this whole big thing. And I just wanted to say "Geez, take a breath, it's a hallway, it's crowded, people are going to bump into each other. Get over it."

Why do you think this happens?

MH: I think if you have a dysfunctional family at home you'll probably fight at school because you're so angry about stuff at home and if someone does one little thing to get you angry then you get really mad and you'll want to fight.

SL: Yeah, because at home you'll have to bundle up all that anger. You'll be so frustrated because you can yell at your parents all you want but no matter what, you can't be right. So you go to school and one person gets in your way and that's who you'll take your anger out on. If you have that much frustration inside you and then one person touches you, you'll explode.

MH is a 15 year old girl
SL is a 15 year old girl

Are there gangs at your school?

GK: Not at my school. But there are some really pathetic wanna-be crews at my school. But [the nearest other high school] is insane. If you look at someone the wrong way there you'll have 20 guys on you after school.

Continued . . .

These two schools are only a few miles apart. What's the difference?

GK: That neighborhood is all Black kids and Mexicans who don't give a damn. Yeah, it's only a stone's throw away, but look at that neighborhood. It is NOT good. This neighborhood is kept clean and so pretty. It's a completely different city, aesthetically, racially, culturally.

Do you know anyone who joined a real gang?

GK: Yeah. A kid I went to [elementary school] with, his little brother. Throughout childhood, it was always us at the beach. He was a great kid, a very funny, very witty, extremely smart kid. But he started hanging out with a bad crowd. Now he steals bikes just to throw them away and steal a new one. He stole MY bike. I've known him for so long. Now he looks up to people who stab and shoot and kill people.

You said he started off as a good, smart kid. What changed?

GK: That neighborhood. Living near the beach. You see all those kids wearing the big white shirts? They're all dressed exactly the same. Those are his role models. This kid's going to prison.

Do you still talk with him?

GK: I see him around. I say "What up?" but I can't understand what he says now. He speaks a completely different language now. It's like (he demonstrates a low mumble of Spanish and English slang that is barely audible).

Last week we had a party for [our graduating class]. And a bunch of kids from [the other neighborhood] showed up. And we said, "Hey, we know you guys, but you can't come in. This is just for our school." So because we don't let them in, they threw bricks into the yard, just missing several kids' heads.

GK is a 17 year old guy

Have you ever been in a fight?

GK: I will not fight unless I absolutely have to.

Have you had to?

GK: Yeah. Over nothing. Like some guy will say, "Why you looking at me?" and I say, "I don't even know you." And they get all in your face and if you say anything back, they start swinging and the minute you defend yourself there are ten of their friends on you.

Are these fights instantaneous or do they build up for a while first?

GK: They're instantaneous. These people don't know you. They don't want to know you. They will start a fight over nothing.

Who is "they"?

GK: You know . . . I've only seen a couple of White kids who act like that. And even they are kind of wanna-bes. They try to act like that, but they rarely back up their words. The only time I really see it it's Hispanic kids. Or Black kids. But not nearly as many Black kids. It's Hispanic kids mostly.

Here in LA there are tensions between several of the Hispanic populations too. Is any of that playing out on campus?

GK: Not really. Usually when there are big race related events it's just Black against Brown.

Where are the Asian kids?

GK: Doing their homework. I sound so racist right now, but it's just the way it is. Yesterday I was in a class. And I found a phone, and I think, "Oh hey, someone lost their phone." And then this Mexican kid, this little gang-banger kid who thinks he's all hard-core says, "Oh Dawg, let me see that." And he took it and puts it in his bag. And I said, "No, Dude, you don't get to do that." And he said, "What are you talking about? You don't know whose phone it is."

Continued . . .

And I said, "You don't either." And he said, "Why are you all in my face?" and I said, "I'm going to return it." And he said, "That's what I'm going to do."

And this girl said, "No, he steals phones and sells them." And I said, "No. You do NOT get to do that this time." And he gets all up in my face, ready to fight me right there in the middle of class.

And I knew there was nothing I could do. What am I supposed to do? He's smaller than me, and I know how they fight. I could have gotten him to the ground. I could have inflicted some serious damage on this kid. But as soon as I do that and leave school I'll have 20 Mexicans on me. AND I'd get suspended for five days. I finally have all A's in my classes and I'd fall behind.

So I get to see this slime ball kid, this piece of shit human being, screw up somebody else's day, by stealing their phone, with all their contacts in it and there was nothing I could do about it. You know how pissed that made me? I wanted to explode.

GK is a 17 year old guy

Have you ever been in a fight?

NI: In ninth grade I was robbed at knifepoint on the way home from school.

I also witnessed a fight on video. Someone had videotaped a fight. And he beat this other kid pretty good. At one point it was just too much to watch. He had this kid pinned to the ground and he was just laying down fists in his face over and over. That right there was one of the things that affected my ideas about fighting. It turned me away from ever fighting.

Most fights start because someone is feeling insecure and they need to [wave] some flag of "This is what I can do!" to show other people.

NI is a 19 year old guy

Tell me about a fight.

HM: My last fight . . . I was drunk. My girlfriend's uncle, he be thinking he's crazy. But I barely met the dude and he's acting all burly. And I told that fool "I think that you think you're tough." And me and that fool, we started getting down. And we knocked over all the food tables. And it was her dad's pad. And he said "Hey, don't be disrespecting my pad." And I don't know what happened, but that fool (his girlfriend's dad) tried to choke me and I grabbed him and I threw that fool down the stairs. And we both tumbled down the stairs and I was bleeding. And her dad said "I don't want him around no more." I said [let's keep fighting] but he didn't want to get down no more.

When you were fighting with your girlfriend's uncle, was that an angry fight, or was it just for entertainment?

HM: It was both. It was fun. I think it was just out of being drunk. And [regarding the second fight] her dad is over it already. He was tripping for a while; he said he was over it, but I could tell he wasn't. But now he's cool.

It sounds like it flared up really fast. Does a fight like that die out just as fast?

HM: It does for me. I just thought it was that we were all drunk. The next day it's "Whatever happened, happened. It's over now."

How about the other people at the party? Were they mad? Did they think you ruined the party?

HM: Yeah, they were mad, but what the hell? They were all drunk too. They were the ones telling me to drink. They kept giving me shots. So in a way it's their fault too. But actually its no ones fault. It was just fun.

Was your girlfriend's take on all this?

HM: I think it attracted her to me more. But she was mad for a while. But she's over it already.

HM is a 19 year old guy

Tell me about a fight.

GA: The last fight I was in, my boyfriend was getting down, and the guy he was getting down with, he pushed me. So I jumped in. He had my boyfriend on the floor, so I started socking him in his back. Then his wife tried to get crazy with me. And then her sister tried to get into it too. So I socked her sister out. And we started getting down and then my boyfriend and that guy stopped fighting and they tried to separate us and then the guy's wife tried to jump me. Then my boyfriend grabbed her and threw her. So then I told him to let me go one-on-one with her. And when I was dragging her, that lady was hanging onto my face. So my face was all scratched up.

Anyone get seriously hurt?

GA: Just my face.

Did your boyfriend appreciate you jumping in?

GA: Well yeah, he'd better! I had his back! He does try to prevent me, but he knows how I am. I have a temper.

GA is a 17 year old girl

Friends and Family

Love is . . . hot pizza made by your mom.

NI is a 19 year old guy

What do your parents not know about you?

NM: My parents don't know a lot about me. I'm not around them a whole lot. I think that a lot of the time they expect me to do bad at something before they expect me to do good. I guess they have reason to think that because I've messed up a lot. But at the same time, I think that makes me work that much harder to do good things for myself.

They don't know a lot about what's going on in my life, like when I got my internships or my jobs or anything. I just say "Oh I have this on this day and something on that day" and they don't really take the time to ask. They don't know how determined I am.

Are you actively keeping secrets, or just keeping your distance?

NM: I don't think it's either. I think that's just the way it's always been. I just kind of do my own thing. There were certain goals that I set for myself and I would just do them. And they just wouldn't ask. When I was living with them it was like "We'll give you food and clothes to wear and money, and things that you need, but that's as far as it goes."

NM is a 17 year old girl

Say something nice about a family member.

DG: My mother's brother and I are close in age. When I was growing up we lived together. He was like my brother. Of all my family he's the one I relate to best. He's like my best friend. He's always pulling through for me. One time when I was [having trouble] I called him and he left work for the day and drove all the way from Orange County to be with me.

DG is a 17 year old girl

Say something nice about your best friends.

CM: Oh, I would just kill myself without them. Really. There are things that I just really wouldn't feel comfortable telling my parents and I can tell my best friends and know that they're not going to judge me for it.

BB: Yeah, I love my best friends because they are always there for me when I need a shoulder to cry on or just to laugh or if I need something crazy to happen I know it will when I'm with them.

CM: Yeah, no matter what your mood they can always cheer you up and they can always tell when it's necessary.

BB: Yeah, it's like we can read each other's minds.

CM is a 17 year old girl
BB is a 16 year old girl

Have you ever had a family member come to your aid?

RD: Yeah, my mom and dad. Basically, my cousin molested me. I went to the police. My parents didn't know, and that was basically like telling them. And they said "Oh we didn't know! And blah blah blah." And "I love you" and "I love you too." And that kind of brought the family together while spreading it out at the same time.

What was your biggest worry in this situation?

RD: The only worry that I had was that our family would never be happy again. I haven't really gone to my cousin's house since that happened. But if I ever do we have to be watched and in a group. It's always going to be awkward.

RD is a 15 year old girl

Tell me something nice about your parents.

DG: I can say something nice about my dad. He was always there. He gave me a lot of chances. And my brother and I are really close, but ever since he got married, I don't really get along with his wife. Before, we used to spend weekends together. But not anymore. That makes me sad.

DG is a 17 year old girl

What do your parents not know about you?

BB: I don't really talk to my parents a lot. I rely on my friends and not my parents. I guess they don't always know what I'm doing all the time, but that's like most teenagers I think.

I go to raves. My parents don't know that I go to raves. I've been raving for about a year and a half. I always say that I'm sleeping at a friend's house and they just accept it. So I go and I come back in the morning and I always wonder, do they know and they're just not saying anything? My parents are really perceptive. They're not just la la la parents who think I'm so good.

So I go and I come home and I feel guilty for lying to them, but it's so fun. But I know that if they knew that I went they wouldn't let me go because they think the rave culture is all about drugs and I don't do drugs. They just don't trust me and that's kind of sad, because otherwise I'd be more open with them if they could trust me. But they don't, so I'm forced to lie.

Are you afraid they'll find out from other friends' parents?

BB: Yeah, every time I go I risk it, because there are pictures everywhere. I know some of my friends' parents know that my parents don't know and they think it's crazy. I think about them finding out from other parents, but it hasn't happened in a year and a half. For all I know they know but just aren't saying anything.

BB is a 16 year old girl

Tell me about your friends.

GK: In the past two years I have grown so much, grown into "myself" because of my friends. I have some of the most beautiful, awesome, amazing friends. And the experiences, the adventures, learning to deal with each other, having to solve our own problems, has matured me in such a dramatic way. I mean really, just an epic blossoming of coming into being. I feel bad for anyone who has to miss out on something like that.

GK is a 17 year old guy

What is going on at school that most adults don't know?

SG: There is a lot that parents don't understand about school. Really, the entire picture parents get from their kids about school is just what you say to them when you come home, which usually consists of "How was your day?" "Fine" and stuff like that. They have no idea what's going on. I'm sure that school has changed a lot since they were around. The biggest thing they are kind of unaware of, or have forgotten since they were kids, is the social hierarchy.

How do you think the social hierarchy has changed?

SG: Well at our school it's the way people divide themselves up into groups. It's not necessarily a bad thing. It's just what we do. I think since our school is so [multicultural], people often just find friends of their own culture. It's not a racist or prejudice thing. It's just things that you have in common with these people. For that reason, since we have such a multi-ethnic and multi-faceted social mix in school, I don't think people fall into niches like geeks and jocks and stuff. It's different from what I can imagine [it was like] when our parents went to school.

SG is an 18 year old guy

What do your parents not know about you?

RR: That they get on my nerves a lot. That they bug a lot. That I like to go by myself a lot and not always be with them.

KL: Yeah. They don't know that I like to hang out with my friends more than stay home.

Does it hurt their feelings when you say you want to be alone?

RR: It hurts my mom. She cries a lot. She says, "I want to be with you. I'm never with you." My parents are divorced. It's kind of weird. She gets kind of jealous because I hang out with my step dad more than with her.

RR is a 15 year old girl
KL is a 15 year old guy

Are you keeping a secret from you parents?

CA: Yes!

RF: Yeah.

CA: My mom looks through all my stuff. It's really annoying. It's an invasion of privacy. She needs to chill down.

Is she looking to try to keep you safe?

CA: No. She's just doing it to be annoying and controlling.

RF: I tell my mom everything.

RF is a 15 year old girl
CA is a 15 year old girl

Has someone come through for you when you needed them?

JC: Never.

SB: Never?

JC: Never.

JC is a 15 year old guy

What do most parents not know?

GK: That's tough, because I assume that they all did the same stuff. But then again, [the world] is a lot different now. Maybe it's all the same stuff. Kids are going to a lot of raves.

I thought that was over.

GK: It's back. It's huge again. Kids are taking a lot of ecstasy.

Ecstasy alone, or mixed with other stuff?

GK: Well it's never by it self any more. It's always mixed with other stuff. [Raves are] mainly dancing. Dancing dancing dancing. Light shows. Kids playing with finger lights. It's actually a really intricate art form what some kids can do with lights. You get white gloves and these little photon lights for each of your fingers. And you can do figure eights and other patters, and it leaves long trails of light. You're basically dancing with light. I do it with glow-poi too.

GK is a 17 year old guy

Have you ever had a chance to help a friend who really needed you?

PO: I don't understand.

Did anyone call you when they were scared or in trouble?

PO: No. Not really. The thing is, they won't be like "Ooooh I need you" or "I need help." It won't be like that.

Tell me about your friends.

PO: I'm really picky. I may talk to you but that doesn't mean I'm your friend. For me to call you a friend is . . . difficult. I mean, just because I know you, and we talk for a while or we kick it for a little bit, I don't consider you a friend. I just consider you someone I know.

Do other people often think you are a friend and then are surprised that you feel differently?

PO: Yeah, it happens a lot. If I'm going to call you a friend I have to know you for a long while. Or there's going to have to be situations where, like you said, "I need you." But I won't say, "I need you." But if you come through, if you're there, yeah, then I'll consider you one. But if you're just there to talk, then I don't consider you a friend.

PO is a 19 year old girl

Say something nice about a family member.

SP: My little sister is five and she makes my mom's bed to make her happy. My older sister and I babysit her when my mom goes to work on Saturdays, and she fixes all our beds, and tells us to close our eyes and then shows us. It's really sweet.

SP is a 14 year old girl

Tell me something nice about the people you live with.

GO: I have two older brothers. They're both out of the house now. One goes to college and the other already graduated, so it's just me and my parents. They are wonderful people, supportive of what I do. They're great parents to me simply because I am the youngest. With the first two kids it was trial and error. Where they screwed up with them, they mold me better. They don't give me as much freedom as I like but in a way it has really helped my academic life. They are looking out for my best interest. I may be dragged kicking and screaming but I'm sure I will thank them.

GO is an 18 year old guy

In your family, who understands you best?

MB: My tia and my grandmother. When I was growing up I used to get kicked out of my house and I'd go on the streets and sometimes I'd go to my grandma's and she'd take care of me. My tia, she supports me too, but back then, if I'd call her, she'd come pick me up, but then take me back to my house where all the problems are. But now she understands that if I don't want to go back then I don't want to go back.

I've been kicked out for six months now and I'm pregnant right now too. I'm five months pregnant. I'm ready to go back but only so my mom can help out with my daughter.

Does your mom want to help out?

MB: Yeah, she wants to help.

And is that help that you actually want?

MB: Yeah, yeah, I guess. I don't know.

MB is an 18 year old girl

Tell me something nice about the people you live with.

TB: There are a lot of people who live at my house, on and off. I have a strange and wonderful family. I have four parent figures that I've had my entire life: parents and step-parents. Despite what people assume, they are all my parents, equally and totally, which is a gift that most people in my position don't get to have. My sibling and step-siblings are . . . well, the amount of comfort that's there, and how intelligent and how beautiful and . . . I've just been absolutely blessed to live with the people that I do.

My sister is super open, so compassionate. She's a woman of extremes. When she's happy, she's so happy that you're scared. When she's mad, its like . . . RUN! Over misunderstandings, she will psychologically scar people. If you mess with her friends or her family, she is ferocious. She's a bit of a princess, but that's part of what makes her who she is. She'll kick your ass in Super Smash AND Guitar Hero.   And my friends won't stop telling me how hot she is. It's kind of disturbing.

TB is a 17 year old guy

What do your parents not know about you?

RF: A lot.

KL: I'm going to skip this one.

RF: My mom doesn't know that I drink a lot of coffee.

RF is a 15 year old girl
KL is a 15 year old guy

Who understands you best at home?

MM: No one.

So who do you rely on?

MM: My best friend. She never lets me down. Two weeks ago I got kicked out of my house and I went to her house.

HG: Yeah. We had her for the entire weekend. We took her to the snow.

When you got kicked out, did your parents know you were with your friend?

MM: Well . . . I called them when I was there [at the snow, a several hour's drive away], so they wouldn't force me to go back.

Why did you get kicked out?

MM: Oh, my mom doesn't like me. I go to my neighbor's house a lot.

MM is a 15 year old girl
HG is a 15 year old girl

Tell me something nice about your parents.

NI: My mother is an excellent cook. She's also a really fun person . . . when she wants to be. She's a good mom. She's good at taking care of people and making sure they are comfortable.

NI is a 19 year old guy

Who do you rely on?

CC: My friend [name withheld]. He always lets me sleep at his place.

MM: And they cuddle, under the blankets. I'm serious. I've seen it.

CC: No!

When you go sleep at his house, is it to get away from your own house, or just to hang out with him?

CC: Just to be with him.

Have you been friends for a long time?

CC: We've been friends since this summer. We just have a lot of things in common.

CC is a 15 year old guy
MM is a 15 year old girl

What do your parents not know about you?

NZ: They basically know everything. I tell my mom everything. She's like a best friend.

Have you ever been afraid to tell her something?

NZ: No. But if I got in trouble at school or got a bad grade, I'd be afraid to tell her that.   She wouldn't be mad, but she'd be disappointed.

How about your dad? Are you as open with him?

NZ: Not that much. It's easier to talk to my mom. I think that's the nature of moms, and plus she's a girl so if you're a girl it's easier.

NZ is a 17 year old girl

Do your parents understand the depth of your friendships?

EA: No.

Why don't they?

EA: Because they're too old.

CA: I'm not really that close to my parents. It's hard to talk to them about stuff. They're so overprotective. They don't really know how to react to anything I tell them.

KG: When I try to tell them anything about my life, they complain about their problems.

DA: Yeah, like you try to tell them something and they go "Well, that's not really important . . . I've had worse stuff happen to me." And I'm like, hey, what happened to the part where you help me? Instead you're just complaining about your problems.

KG: You've got to be careful what you tell parents because they always come up with an argument.

DA: Yeah. Every time.

EA is 14 year old guy
KG is a 14 year old girl
DA is a 14 year old girl
CA is a 15 year old girl

What do your parents not know about you?

KG: My mom doesn't know that I can be very deep. She doesn't know all my talents. She doesn't know me . . . like me when I'm with my friends. It's just really difficult to talk to her like I talk to my friends.

Continued . . .

108

CA: My mom doesn't know that I have guy friends. She doesn't want me to have guy friends because she thinks guy friends lead to boyfriends. I always tell my guy friends, "When my mom comes to pick me up, don't hug me good-bye."

Does she think that a guy friend is automatically a boyfriend?

CA: Totally. And one time, I have this friend who is gay, and he didn't know that my mom was watching and he hugged me and I got in the car my mom says "So you got a boyfriend now!?" And I'm like "Mom. He's gay."

Several girls at once: Ooohhhh burn!

CA: Yeah, and she's all "uuuuuuhhhh."

KG is a 14 year old girl
CA is a 15 year old girl

Tell me something nice about your family.

MH: When I'm in Georgia at my grandparent's house, I have a room there. When I'm there I feel so happy all the time. That's where I was born, and that's where I lived with my parents before my dad died. So whenever I'm there I feel happy because I feel like my dad is with me.

Do you feel like you have access to him? Do you talk to him?

MH: Sometimes.

Do you think that's related to God, or is that a direct line to your dad?

MH: I think it's my dad.

MH is a 15 year old girl

Do you have love in your life?

GK: I have so much love. Maybe not romantic love, but the word "love" means so much. First off, I love my parents. And my parents love me. And there is so much love in this house that I have been blessed with. And that really helps, because no matter what's going on outside of this, I always have this to return to.

I love my dog. I love my friends. I have certain friends that I can be completely selfless with. Me and one friend in particular, we are drastically friends. We could live together for long periods of time. We can wear each other's clothes, share food. And it's so nonchalant, like "Oh, this is mine? Then it's yours too."

There are times, weekends, where our wallets will merge, because if there's something either of us is going to buy, then it's automatically for both of us.

Does that ever lead to conflict?

GK: Oh yeah, certainly.

How do you deal with that?

We do it incredibly well! We are very mature about our conflict resolution. Like a few weeks ago, I was having a really rough time, and I was just really irritable. And I was ragging on him non-stop. And he called me on it and said "Dude, I can't deal with this any more. I just want to knock you out." And I had the worst day after that! Then I wrote him a two-page email, about what I treasure about our friendship and told him, "You are the only person I can really [be myself with], and if we don't solve this, I am going to die." And [after he read it] he said, "There is no way I could tell you how happy that made me."

GK is a 17 year old guy

Pride, Respect and Choices

I'm proud of how I can make people laugh
and cheer them up when they are sad.

CA is a 15-year-old girl

What is your biggest responsibility?

SG: My biggest responsibility is to experience as much of life as I can and meet as many people as I can and share experiences. I think that sharing experiences and interacting with as many people as we can, slowly but surely brings about a deeper understanding of the world.

SG is an 18 year old guy

What is your biggest responsibility?

NI: My biggest responsibility is . . . myself. I have to exercise self-control and really take care of myself. I feel like I'm really watching my own back now, because a lot of the situations I'm in are very unstable.

The economy is so terrible right now, and it's been hard for a lot of people to find work or make a living.

I'm prone to sort of running off and hiding from my problems. What I'm working on right now is training myself, mentally and physically, to do what I need to do to take care of my future. It's been going well. I'm making slow progress. I've had problems with smoking too much marijuana. I definitely need to alter the amount of time it takes up in my life.

I've been going to community college, going back in the winter. And I'm working on a couple of different music projects. I'm trying to discipline myself, training myself to know what to do with what slots of times, like how to spend my days efficiently and get things done.

NI is a 19-year-old guy

Who do you respect?

GO: I don't really care too much about what other people think about me. We all are self conscience in some respects but I've certainly felt less so [than other people do]. Of course I'll conform to certain things in my group of friends, but in general I wear what I want and I do what I want. I haven't really had to make any choices that sacrifice that, other than school, which is not my choice. I kind of have to do that and study a bunch of crap.

I respect intellectuals, the idea of thinking, of thought, of questioning, of not taking anything at face value and coming to your own conclusions. I respect people who seek out experiences. And I respect people who try to do good in the world.

I have respect for old people not because they're old, well . . . yeah, because they're old. I respect them simply for the fact that they've experienced so much. And that's something they will always have on me . . . until I get old . . . and they're dead.

GO is an 18 year old guy

Who do you respect?

NA: I respect people who take action to be helpful, on a stranger-on-the-street level.

NA is a 19 year old girl

What would you like people to know?

GK: Give us a little more credit for our ability to solve our own problems and take care of ourselves.

GK is a 17 year old guy

What is your biggest responsibility?

TB: My biggest responsibility is . . . well, that's why I quit smoking pot. I couldn't remember what I was supposed to do! Actually, my biggest responsibility is to try to spend each moment acknowledging that it's a passing moment, and that the people that I share it with should never be [taken for granted].

TB is a 17 year old guy

What is tagging?

TB: Tagging has absolutely no artistic value. Graffiti on the other hand—I love graffiti. It's a very difficult, beautiful art form that has a lot of respect.   And you have to appreciate the conditions under which a lot of this art was created. It's incredibly difficult.

Tagging on the other hand, is the human equivalent of dogs pissing on things. You make up a stupid name for yourself, get a permanent marker and go around town writing your name on things. Then people from other crews cross out your name and write their own name. Like on a stop sign, like you can "own" that stop sign. It's ridiculous.   And then they meet up sometime and say "Hey you crossed me out!" and they get in a huge brawl over nothing.

TB is a 17 year old guy

What are you proud of?

MB: I'm always proud. I'm proud of the fact that I work hard. Like, they don't have to ask me twice [at work]. I do my job. Some of these other kids make faces and whine, but I don't. I'm proud of that.

MB is an 18 year old girl

Who do you respect?

SG: I respect people who have a direction in life. It really doesn't matter what you're doing, [as long as you] are not drifting aimlessly. You actually have a plan and you have motivation. You know how to get from point A to point B. That earns my respect. It doesn't matter what you're doing, even things I disagree with.

Do your friends respect you?

SG: Respect is such a weird term. It's taught in every classroom. It's the number one rule that you are supposed to give your teacher respect. I think the word is kind of thrown around. I think it's something that should be earned. In first or second grade, they post class rules, like "Respect yourself" and "Respect your neighbors." I don't like that. It's a word that's thrown around too much.

I like to think my friends respect me but sometimes I screw up. Sometimes I act a certain way in front of my friends to protect my integrity and hope they still respect me. Additionally, my parents respect me more and more as I become less of a burden and more of an adult. The more independence I have, the more respect they give me.

SG is an 18 year old guy

What is written on your chest? (Big black letters in felt pen are visible at her collar.)

HG: It says "ugly."

Who put that there?

HG: Me.

HG is a 14-year-old girl

What are you proud of?

HM: I'm proud of the way I am. A lot of people are back stabbers and two faced. I'm not like that. I'm not going to go behind your back. And I'm smart too.

HM is a 19-year-old guy

What are you proud of?

GA: I'm proud of who I am today. I don't care what anyone else says. I know who I am and I know what I'm about and I don't have to prove myself to anybody else. I know what I used to be and I know what I am now and I'm really proud of that.

GA is a 17-year-old girl

What is your biggest responsibility?

GO: I want to work toward living a simpler life for more people. Living within our means. Returning to a more simple lifestyle. People are going say, "Oh that's going be hard." But I would disagree and say that it would actually make us happier. I think that our society is such a complex thing.   And our government brings about more complexities, and more things to worry about.   I think that by simplifying, removing all of these complexities, well not all, but certainly some, we can be happier.   And I think that's one of my responsibilities, to work toward that goal.

GO is an 18 year old guy

Do you do any drugs?

MB: I got into drugs in the past, but it just made me feel stupid. Like I would think I was reading, but I was actually just staring [at the book]. I didn't like that.

MB is an 18-year-old girl

Have you ever been the one to stop your friends from doing something dangerous?

PO: Yeah. Many times.

There's this one spot where my friends and me used to kick it, and mostly I'm the only girl there. Sometimes there are other girls there, but they're just there to be with a guy. They're not there for the same reason I'm there. One time some fools from [another neighborhood] came by and we were like "What the hell?" It turned out these guys were there to jack my homeboy's house. And we got there and they saw us coming and they jumped back in the car and started shooting. They drove away. But we knew the car now. And then later that same night we see the car again.   And so my boys, they start getting ready to . . . to . . . you know . . . if anything happens.

And I got this feeling. You know when you get a feeling that something's wrong? And I argued with them for a long time not to do anything. And then the car came down our street and they were prepared and in position. [she makes a gesture of cocking a large gun.] It's a dead end street. And I kept saying, "Don't do anything. Something's not right." And they kept saying "It's them. It's the same car." And the car came down our street and we see in the windows it was a bunch of girls and they were lost!

And my boys were all "What the hell!?" and I said, "See I told you, it's not them." It was just a feeling, but I was right.

PO is a 18 year old girl

118

I've been sober for the past 30 days,
which is the longest time in a period of two years.
I feel wonderful.

TB is a 17-year-old guy

Why do you think people smoke weed?

SP: They have problems, or they want to be cool.

Recently my friend just got back from a suspension. They got caught drinking, which is terrible. She was hanging out with the wrong crowd. Like, when we look over at their table [at lunch] all of the people are people that you really wouldn't want to know. They're really creepy.

As soon as I started high school, everything was new to me. Like there's this guy who comes into class and his eyes are all blood shot and he comes into class and then sometimes just goes right back out.

I see a lot of people with acne and I asked my health teacher and she said most people get acne because it's in their genetics or it's because they smoke. My friend, she didn't have acne before. I've known her since elementary. And now her face is filled with acne. And another friend told me that she smokes. Her face used to be really pretty, like nothing was on her face. I don't want that.

SP is a 14-year-old girl

What are you proud of?

EA: My musical talent. I play trumpet, guitar and bass. I actually have a trumpet and a guitar. But I really want a bass.

SB: Is your family proud of your musical ability?

EA: Half and half. I'm doing good in school right now so that leads me to my guitar and trumpet. My parents like that I play trumpet. I've been doing it since fourth grade.

EA is a 14-year-old guy

What are you proud of?

CA: I'm proud that I can wear what ever the heck I want whenever the heck I want to. That's what I hate about my mom. Every time I walk through the room it's "What are you wearing?!" That's why I'm really careful when she's there. I hide what ever I wear. Like this morning I was hiding behind the kitchen counter and I'd walk this way every time she walked that way so she wouldn't see my tights. Then she unexpectedly walked up behind me and she [makes a shocked face] and she said "You know what? I'm not going to say anything"

KG: She just said something!

CA: I know! I mean I'm proud that I can be what I am with out going "Oh what do people think of my hair? Oh my god what are people thinking of me? Oh my god." And my mom, I hear her say "You shouldn't wear that to school. People are going to make fun of you." And I'm like "You actually think I'm that weak?"

CA is a 15-year-old girl
KG is a 14 year old girl

Have you ever had to be the voice of reason for your friends?

SP: One of my best friends told me that another friend of ours was going to drink. And we told her not to, and she said that she [already decided not to] because she knew that we would get mad. She didn't do it because of us, and we were happy.

SP is a 14-year-old girl

What are you proud of?

SP: I'm proud of what I am. Like all the stuff I've done. I think I've made good choices, nothing dumb that I would regret later on.

Did your parents teach you that or is that the way you are naturally?

SP: My parents [provide me with] a good environment, but I think I would have good judgment naturally.

SP is a 14-year-old girl

Is it important that you match a certain style at school?

RR: I am a freak. I come to school wearing . . . crazy stuff. Remember I wore a tutu?

DA: Yeah. That was great. You looked so cute.

RR: I wore a crown one day.

How do people react when you do that?

RR: They call me a freak and say "Why are you wearing that!" and I say "Because it's freaking awesome!"

DA: Nice!

RR: Yeah, it's like, what? I'm supposed to care what YOU think?

RR is a 15-year-old girl
DA is a 14 year old girl

Tell me about your friends

MB: I don't really have friends. I don't really like to kick it with bitches because they're all drama and shit. They back stab, that's all they do. I've lost trust in generally everybody. I tried to be friends with lots of bitches, but I've been back stabbed and I've been jumped and it's hard. That's why I don't really socialize with any one.

How about now that you're pregnant?

MB: Well, I tried to stop fighting once I got pregnant, 'cause I have a really bad temper. And it's hard for me, because that's what I'm used to doing. That's the way I defend myself.

If you're in a fight with another girl, and she knows you're pregnant, does that change the way the fight goes?

MB: They don't care. I was in a situation where this bitch tried to mess with me, and she knows I'm pregnant, right? And it's hard, because I'm trying to work on myself, trying to not be so violent and she's trying to push my buttons. I just try to control it. I just want my baby to come out healthy, you know? I don't want any more bullshit, you know? I haven't really fought in about a year, ever since I started working here [a facility for at-risk youth]. These people gave me a shot, a chance to start over, so I took it seriously. I really started changing here. I really try to work on myself. But there are people here who really push me, and I just have to take off, and cool down.

How hard is that . . . to remove yourself from a situation that would ordinarily launch you into a fight?

MB: It's hard . . . it's SO hard, because I want to kill the bitch.

Does it get easier with practice?

MB: Yeah . . . and I have somebody to talk to now. When I really want to do something, I just let it all out inside the room [counselor's office]. But sometimes, when I just really feel like I want to beat them up I do take off and I try to cool off. I'm trying to control it more and more. But what really helps now is I just try to think about my daughter.

MB is an 18-year-old girl

Money and Jobs

I want to work at Hot Dog on a Stick.
I like the costume.

KS is a 15 year old girl

Do you make money?

GS:　I work at a restaurant. I'm cashier. I count the money. That's a big responsibility. I work seven or eight hours a week.

Do you feel like you are paid what the job is worth?

GS:　Kind of and kind of not. I wish I could get a raise, but it's my grandparent's restaurant, so I'm not going to complain.

Do you like your job?

GS:　Not really, because I don't want to be in the food industry. I want to be more into retail merchandise, because I'm into fashion.

GS is a 17 year old girl

Do you have a job?

CL:　No, but I want one. I want a job so I can have MY money instead of always asking my mom for money.

AR:　I'd like to work at a clothes store.

Do boys or girls have more employment opportunities?

CL:　I think girls work more.

AR:　My family owns motels, and I live in one. It's a very interesting life.

CL:　My parents own laundromats.

CL is a 16 year old girl
AR is a 17 year old girl

Do you have a job?

GO: I've been a camp counselor at a camp for little kids for years. I save my money and I've bought some big-ticket items, like guitars.

GO is an 18 year old guy

What are people buying and selling at school?

RD: There's this thing where there's Kool-Aid and gummy worms. And people actually make a lot of money off them. It's really funny. They charge a dollar a bag.

What are you talking about?

RD: They get the big bag of gummies at Smart and Final or at Costco. And you buy sandwich bags and Kool-Aid. You toss the gummy worms with Kool-Aid powder.

SE: Some people do chili powder.

Does the administration know this is going on?

RD: If you get caught selling, it's a suspension. But if you don't get caught . . . well . . .

SE: And there's drugs. There's always drugs at school.

RD: And clothes and shoes.

SE: Yeah, some people buy shoes and when they don't want them anymore, especially if they're expensive shoes, they sell them at school. Especially shoes that they don't make anymore, like limited edition Nikes and Jordans.

RD is a 15 year old girl
SE is a 15 year old girl

Tell me about a job.

SG: All the best stories come from camp. I was a camp counselor for years. Working with four and five year olds is great. It's tough. It's really hard, but it's a great experience. You learn a lot. You become a much more patient person. Especially when you just look at them and want to strangle them.

SG is an 18 year old guy

Are there good jobs available to teenagers?

AR: I have a few friends who are strippers. The actually make a lot of money.

Do they work private parties or clubs?

AR: Clubs. They're seniors, they're 18, so they can work. Their parents don't know. They think they are doing after school classes. They make thousands.

What are their working conditions?

AR: I don't know . . . I've never been to the clubs where they work.

How did you feel when they told you?

AR: Well, I said "Oh that's awesome" but it's sad, because kids want their own money, but you have to do really bad choices to get the money, and that sucks. Instead of doing a responsible job . . . because when you think about it, being a stripper is degrading.

GS: Yeah, its degrading but you don't have to stay for long hours and then clean up after people for eight dollars an hour. It's a better job than a restaurant where you have to wait on people and clean up after people.

AR is a 17 year old girl
GS is a 17 year old girl

If some friends are getting money from parents and some are not, do you think they should share?

GK: Yes, but people are stingy.   Like right now, I'm not getting any money from my parents. My friends get 40 dollars a week for allowance. And I'm like, oh God, I would kill for 40 dollars.

Does that monetary difference put a strain on friendships?

GK: Oh God yes. It's hard not to get envious, but sometimes I get genuinely really mad, because they've never done yard work before. With my richer friends, yeah, there's huge envy. And they're not the friends who share. With my friends who never have money, when [one of us] does get money, it's automatically "our" money, because we go have fun with it. But my friends who get 40 dollars a week and don't even clean up their own rooms, they're like "What are you talking about? No, this is MY money."

I think if everyone had to really pull their own weight, if everyone had to start from nothing, it would be a different world.

GK is a 17 year old guy

Are you using credit cards?

PO: Yeah, I used to. When I barely turned 18 I got one credit card. Then, I don't know how it happened that I accidentally applied for another card. So I was using one card and within two months I [maxed it out]. It was only $500. So I got a bill for that, and then I got a bill for the other credit card. I wasn't planning on using it, but then I thought, if I'm going to get a bill I might as well use it. So then I [maxed out] that one too.

So how much credit card debt do you have now?

PO: About a thousand dollars. Well, a thousand and a bit

PO is an 18 year old girl

How do you make money? How do you spend most of your money?

SG: I teach piano to little kids. It's really frustrating working with little kids. I do a lot of work with kids not because I'm good with them, but because I'm NOT good with them. I force myself to because it's a skill that I'm sure is good to have. It would be terrible to be creepy around kids. I'm getting better at it. Now, actually the biggest burden is talking with the parents. I'll be teaching the kid and the parent will be hovering over me trying to teach me how to teach them. But it is a rewarding job.

So yeah, I private tutor math to a couple kids on the weekdays. I teach piano on the weekends. It's fairly good money. I am saving a lot of it for the summer. I want to travel in South America. I put away half of what I make each week. The rest I will spend on food during the week and on the weekend on alcohol, weed or more hardcore drugs. I don't know. Mainly drugs. I like drugs. I don't really go to the movies or stuff like that. A lot of stuff that I do with my friends is free. I don't really need to pay for anything when I hang at someone's house.

There's camping. Camping costs money. We all don't go to Disneyland every weekend. I am sure if we had a lot more money our lives wouldn't be that different. I don't usually miss out on anything for lack of money. So yeah, drugs and food. That's what I spend my money on.

SG is an 18 year old guy

Are people buying and selling stuff at school?

KG: Well, there's gummy worms . . . and drugs.

EA: And right now there are Girl Scout cookies!!!

KG: Yeah! Its Girl Scout cookie time!

Continued . . .

131

Are pharmaceuticals being sold?

KG: Yeah, some, but it's mainly weed.

Where does it come from?

KG: The people I know who sell it get it from their parents.

Do the parents know?

EA: No.

KG: Are you kidding? Of course the parents know.

What's your opinion about this?

KG: I think it's not my business. It's not something I'm into, but I'm like, OK.

Do your friends offer it to you?

EA: No. I'm not popular, so no one offers it to me.

It's connected to popularity?

EA: Of course.

JC: They don't offer it to me, because they already know I would say "no."

EA: People get popular by selling it.

KG: Another way it [gets to us] is that lots of older people, like over 18, hang out with high schoolers and it just works its way down to people like us.

KG is a 14 year old girl
EA is a 14 year old guy
JC is a 16 year old guy

How do you make money?

RD: I don't really make money. Sometimes I'll ask my mom for money but my family is not that rich. We're barely making it, so I don't like to ask.

Do you need money throughout the day?

SE: Oh yes. But I just try to avoid situations where I need money.

RD: It's hard for me, because I like to buy a lot of things. I'm a shopaholic. I recently asked my grandpa for money. He gave me a hundred dollars. I spent all that money on shopping. He thinks I'm going to pay him back and I have no way of paying him back. It's kind of messed up, but I don't know what to do at this point. I really WANT to repay him.

What did you tell him the money was for?

RD: Charity. I know. That's bad.

RD is a 15 year old girl
SE is a 15 year old girl

Do you have a job?

NM: For a while, I was working at Pink Berry, and I had internships. Now I'm a receptionist at a martial arts studio.

SB: Do you make enough to support yourself?

NM: Yes, but I have to start saving because I'm going to move soon.

NM is a 17 year old girl

How do you make money?

HM: I have a job.

Is it enough to support you?

HM: It's enough money for what I need. There's stuff that I want, but if I can't afford it then I can't afford it. But I have everything that I need.

Sometimes people try to get crazy here, like "This is MY hood." And I just have to go (he makes a gesture of waving someone off). And these fools are in cars. But a lot of people come through here, you know? And I have a lot of enemies, because of my 'hood. But I need to be here. My job is here.

Do you still feel tempted sometimes to go make money in other ways, other than your job?

HM: I can't. There are so many police here now. It's too complicated. Like before, you could go make money, but now it's too hard.

HM is a 19 year old guy

What is being bought and sold at school?

JH: Candy. Some people come to school with a big [satchel or gym bag] and it's full of candy and chocolate. And throughout the day they are selling it for a buck or two. They make really good money if you think of what it costs to buy a case of Snicker's at Smart and Final. But if security comes around they usually have a friend hold their cash. If security thinks you are selling, they'll ask you to empty your pockets and if you have a ton of singles and a bunch of candy they know you're selling. But if you only have a little money on you they can't prove anything.

JH is a 14 year old girl

134

Do you have a job?

MB: I work in an office. I get paid ok for my position. I was hoping for more. But it's all right. I'm just being patient. I'm trying to be better. I have an easy way to make more money, but I know it's not the right thing. That's why I'm trying to discipline myself and learn and I'm not slinging rock anymore and I'm not making any dirty money anymore. I'm trying to earn it the right way, trying to live a decent life.

What about your friends who are still making money selling on the street? Do they have comments for you?

MB: No. They have respect for me. They don't really look down on me. They wish that they could do like I'm doing. But they can't. It's just a lifestyle that they are stuck to.

Do you make enough to support yourself?

MB: Yeah. This place has flexible hours so I can go to school at the same time. I want to finish school and from there I want to go to college to be a nurse.

Why nursing?

MB: I guess because my dad wanted to be a doctor and he didn't get to do that, so I want to do that for him.

MB is an 18 year old girl

Where are you getting money?

EA: I don't get any money.

DA: Me either.

Continued . . .

But I see chips and soda in your hands right now. Where did you get the money for that?

CA: Well, I do chores and stuff.

KL: Yeah, we do chores.

RR: Not me. I just get it.

DA: Well, sometimes when I ask [for money] they say yes, but mostly it's "noooooooo."

What do you do when you're with friends who have money when you don't?

CA: I steal their food.

How do you spend your money?

KL: Burritos. Food. Clothes. Books.

Do you need money at school?

RR: Not really. We just buy worthless stuff.

CA: I get 10 dollars a week. And I'm good at saving.

What are you saving for?

CA: Nothing specific. I just save it. And when I want to spend it I spend it.

Do you have a checking account or use credit cards?

No. It's just cash in pocket. But I have a friend who has a debit card.

EA is a 14 year old guy
CA is a 15 year old girl
KL is a 15 year old guy
RR is a 15 year old girl
DA is a14 year old girl

Do you have a job or do you get allowance?

EA: I find spare change. And I take the bus so I have to make change, so I keep the change and save it up.

Do you have enough money for what you need through out the day?

EA: Kind of.

You take the city bus to get to this school? What neighborhood do you live in?

EA: Downtown LA. I'm here on permit.

RR: Me too.

KL: Me too.

EA is a 14 year old guy
RR s a 15 year old girl
KL is a 15 year old guy

Has money ever dramatically affected an event with a friend?

GO: It was last year. I have no problem lending friends money. But I have one friend who borrowed money a lot. He would pay me back eventually, but I got fed up with him owing me money. It was quickly resolved. It was a stupid argument over money for drugs. Drugs and money are superficial things and it's stupid for it to cause a fight. We're both smart enough and proud enough to eventually overcome the problem and work it out. It was short.

GO is an 18 year old guy

Do you have a job?

TB: I don't have a job. I'm useless.

Do you feel useless?

TB: Sometimes. I held a really god job for a long time. At the time, I had a lot of contempt for what I thought I got out of it. So I left it. But now, when I look back on it, I have nothing but appreciation for the things I learned doing it.

TB is a 17 year old guy

What is your job?

NA: I've been working here (a restaurant) since I was 17.

Is your income here enough to sustain you?

NA: Sometimes it is and sometimes it isn't.

What do you do when its not?

NA: Nothing, I just wait for my next check.

Are you using credit cards?

NA: No. I just have a debit card. I try not to waste my money.

NA is an 18 year old girl

Do you have a job?

SP: Not now, but I worked last summer at a jewelry shop in the mall. It was one of those little booths.

Do you need money throughout the day?

SP: Yeah, like if I want to buy a cookie or something.

How do you get money?

SP: My parents give it to me. It's a regular amount each time. And I do my chores of course.

What is being bought and sold at school?

SP: Gummy worms are everywhere.

How much do they cost?

SP: Depends. If it's a big bag it's two dollars. If it's small bag, it's one dollar. But I personally don't like them. It's disgusting.

Are there other things for sale?

SP: Well, people bake cakes for friends. But that's not usually for sale. People do sell their stuff. And people get caught. You get suspended or expelled, depends. My sister's friend sold weed and he got expelled.

What's your take on this?

SP: I think it's ridiculous. I think it's pointless. Why would you waste your life for a couple of bucks?

Are people selling pharmaceuticals?

SP: Not that I've seen.

SP is a 14 year old gir

How do you make money and how do you spend it?

NI: It's hard for a teenager to find comfortable employment. And especially for me because I prefer freedom over having to labor.   So if I'm not in a job, which I'm typically not, I make money by selling old possessions, or by coming up with schemes like washing cars or detailing cars. Sometimes I go to the 99 cent store and find good deals on things and resell them to people. Hustling, if you will.

I have, in the past, sold drugs, not illicit drugs, but usually marijuana. I don't find its effects harmful or detrimental. I don't think it's a drug that ruins people's lives, so I don't have any problem morally selling it. I sometimes do tasks and favors for family and friends.

NI is a 19 year old guy

How do you spend your money?

GO: I usually save my money, but if I can have new experiences, or do things with my friends, money becomes less of an object. I'll spend more if it means new experiences and new people.

GO is an 18 year old guy

School

Ms S. helped me a lot. I just graduated.
She's been my best teacher ever.
I went into the hospital and when I came back
she stayed with me until 8:00 in the nights
to help me finish the work to graduate.

DG is an 18 year old girl

Tell me about your favorite class.

JH: Sometimes in Mr. G's class someone has to sing me a happy song.

What do you mean?

JH: Apparently in that class I look mad or something.

SL: You DO! Oh my God. Every time I walk past that class you're like (she makes a really grumpy face).

JH: Yeah, so Mr. G asks the guy who sits next to me to sing me a happy song.

JH is a 14 year old girl
SL is a 14 year old girl

Tell me about an excellent teacher.

HM: I never had a good teacher. But maybe that's because I used to never pay attention. But Mr. F, he's a good teacher. He teaches you about stuff that you never think about, you know? Like history. Like that dude Martin Luther King? He plays that speech and you trip out. That class is excellent.

When the environment is better, you are a better student?

HM: Yeah. Definitely. That teacher really motivated me, and now I'm going to graduate in June.

HM is a 19 year old guy

What do most adults not know about school?

GO: Parents are aware, but not conscience of it on the level that we are, about how much pressure we're under to do well in school so you can get a good job. It can cause a lot of anxiety and depression. There's not enough encouragement to do what you WANT to do.

Our parents went through school. They know what kind of crap we have to go through. For the most part, school is a load of crap. We should be finding out what we're interested in doing. Most kids don't know what they want to do later in life, but almost every one knows what they DON'T want to do. By about mid high school, you get an idea of what you want to study, simply because of the intrinsic rewards of learning about it.

I think we should have greater choices earlier on in school. There shouldn't be such a core curriculum of required classes if so many of these classes you know you'll never be interested in using later in your life.

GO is an year old guy

What would you change about school?

TB: I'd have teachers work more hands-on with the students. When a teacher has five or six classes a day, each with about 30 or 40 kids in some places, it's very difficult for them to build relationships. The amount of barriers that are put between teachers and students in public schools leaves everyone feeling untouched. Whereas in private schools that I've attended there are maybe 15 kids in a class. Teachers have the ability to actually challenge themselves by challenging their students.

TB is a 17 year old guy

Tell me about your favorite teacher.

TR: My favorite teacher was Miss F. But recently she's been really moody and bitchy.

PA: My favorite teacher is Mr. P. He's a drama teacher. He's really cool. He lets us out early because sometimes he has to do things. But he's a really good teacher. If you just mess up a little bit he'll say "Oh let me help you with this." And he owns a motorcycle. Which is really cool.

TR is a 17 year old girl
PA is a 17 year old girl

Tell me about your favorite teacher.

HG: Miss C, the computer teacher. She's really chill. I guess you could call her a pushover, but we don't do anything bad.

ZR: Yeah, we don't take advantage of her because we know she's nice. She gives us space to do our own work.

MM: My teacher looks like a goat. That's why he's my favorite.

HG is a 14 year old girl
ZR is a 14 year old guy
MM is a 15 year old girl

Tell me about your favorite teacher.

AA: My favorite teacher right now is Ms. M. because she's young and she understands things a lot more. She's the cheerleading coach as well, so she's really peppy. Sometimes she can be annoying, but she's a really good teacher. She works out of the book, but also doesn't work out of the book. We do lots of labs and she tries to explain things as much as possible. We do a lot of projects, which really helps me.

AA is a 15 year old girl

Are you really involved at school?

GK: No, because I don't really care that much about school. I have my group of friends, and I try to not look at anyone else, because a lot of things make me really mad at school.

Like what?

GK: Like the way people work. Like kids who all dress exactly the same and they don't even know why they do it. They just do it because everyone else does it.

Do you feel like you dress in a sort of uniform?

GK: I guess I've adopted the "anti-uniform" uniform. I've stopped thinking about it. I just throw on whatever is in my closet.

GK is a 17-year-old guy

Tell me about starting middle school.

SL: When I first went to middle school, I wasn't scared at all. Yes, there are 1700 kids in this school. But that just means there are so many new people to hang out with.

MH: I was really scared on the first day, because I had gone to a Catholic school before where we were all in one room. It was really scary at first, but I made a lot of new friends. Catholic school was really protected. People were on top of us all the time. But then in [public] middle school we had a longer leash. We could do more stuff.

Do you miss that sense of protection and that small school feeling?

MH: No! I love the public school so much more than the Catholic school.

SL is a 14 year old girl
MH is a 15 year old girl

Have you ever had an excellent teacher?

MB: I'm going to graduate this year. I never thought I was going to get this far, because I never really went to school. And when I did go I had the worst teachers. They would talk crap about me and put me down and tell me I was stupid. I go to a charter school now.

What's different about this school?

MB: It's a lot about the teacher's attitudes. I feel like they are really paying attention to me and they really want me to do something with my life. And that really gives me inspiration.

MB is an 18 year old girl

What is your favorite class?

MM & HG: MATH!! (said together)

MM is a 15 year old girl
HG is a 14 year old girl

What are you doing now that you've graduated?

NI: I'm really happy to be out of high school. I have a better respect for my education because I'm paying for it myself now. And I feel like I'm working toward an ultimate end now. And I'm finally getting a chance to work on some of my passions, which I never had time for before.

NI is a 19-year-old guy

Where do you live?

ZR: I live in Hollywood.

CC: I live in downtown LA.

So why are you going to school here in this neighborhood?

ZR: The schools around where I live are not that great.

How would your life be different if you'd gone to your neighborhood school?

CC: I'd be a cholo by now.

ZR is a 14 year old guy
CC is a 15 year old guy

Is your academic life important to you?

GO: When I'm going through a lot of things in life, when stuff starts going down and stuff gets hectic, I always find myself putting schoolwork as the number one priority simply because, in my limited scope of what's going on or what's going to happen to me, I kind of cling to the idea that if I do well in school, I'll do well in life. I know that's not necessarily true but I've got to hold onto some belief. I put that responsibility down on myself.

GK: That's interesting, because I'm just the opposite. When stuff gets really hectic and I start to second-guess myself, I distance myself from school.

GO is an 18 year old guy
GK is a 17 year old guy

Tell me about your favorite teacher.

BB: My favorite teacher is my math teacher, Mr. D. That's because he makes sure that you get it. He goes up to every student individually in the class who he knows has trouble with a certain topic and he'll ask if you get it and if you don't he'll stick on the subject until you get it. And he's always there for individual help. And he's really funny.

CM: I would hate that. I hate to be pointed out and asked, "What's wrong?"

BB: Well I'm the kind of person who really likes that. I need to be able to ask questions constantly and have a teacher paying attention to me, wanting me to understand.

CM: I can ask questions but I don't like it when he's in front of the class teaching a lesson and he points me out by name and asks, "Do YOU get it?"

BB: Well, it's not like he's pointing you out like you're stupid. He just wants you to do well. He cares. It shows he actually cares.

CM: I know. I still wouldn't like it. Would you like it?

NM: I don't like being put on the spot, but I like it when teachers show that they are not just doing their job, that what they do goes beyond what they are paid to do. I like seeing that they care about each individual student, but I don't like being called out on. I like when I feel that I can talk to a teacher outside of class at any time. But I wouldn't want to be called on. I get what you're saying.

BB: Well, he feels like a friend more than a teacher. So it doesn't feel as weird.

BB is a 16 year old girl
CM is a 17 year old girl
NM is a 17 year old girl

Do you think your high school experience is typical?

TB: I went to [two different public schools very near each other]. They were completely different. One school was completely used to having to deal with delinquency and crime so it adapted in its own way. And then you head a little bit north and you're talking about more economically stable neighborhoods. You're talking about more control. So the social hierarchy is going to be different. So you can never answer, "What is the average high-schooler like?"

TB is a 17-year-old guy

If you could change school, what would you change?

AA: I would change the levels. In the honors class I'm in right now, I feel kind of out of place because I can keep up, but not as easy as everyone else. And in the regular classes I'm in it's kind of like "Everyone here is really stupid." I guess more levels or no levels. Throughout the day I'm either struggling or bored.

AA is a 15 yearold girl

How much of your day is spent waiting?

KS: I think about five minutes for each period. We're freshmen, so we all don't want to get in trouble. But [back in 8th grade], it took everyone about ten minutes to quiet down. But the teachers are always ready.

KS is a 15 year old girl

What is your favorite class?

CC: P.E.

HG: You should see him run. It's so pretty. He's like a horse.

CC is a 15 year old guy
HG is a14 year old girl

Tell me about leaving school.

NM: I left high school after my freshman year. Ninth grade was such a difficult for me. I was depressed all the time. I was crying and I was angry all the time. It's true that once you start ditching, it's hard to get back. You can either sleep in and go do something that you want, or get up early and go do something that you don't want.

I didn't hate school; but I hated the people at my school. I mean . . . the people that age, I couldn't relate to them. The things that they talked about or cared about, I really couldn't care less about. So it was just me at school being sad.

After I ditched a lot, I'd lost a lot of credit. So I signed myself up for a home school course. Then when I was 16, I took a test called the CHSPE. Passing this test proves that you would have gotten a certain score on the SATs. So I took the test and passed it and that made it legal for me to not be in school.

And then I got a job, and I was working a lot, since I had all this time that I wasn't in school. And in January I started college!

MN is a 17-year-old girl

How much of your day is spent waiting?

Oh my God. If I could do school at my own pace I would have graduated years ago. I get into class and I have to wait for the teacher to show up. Sometimes they're not even there. Then I have to wait for all the kids to shut up. I have to wait for people to understand, and then I have to wait for the slow people to ask a bunch of questions. Then I have to wait for the teacher to hand stuff out and I have to wait for ... everything.

It's ridiculous. I have one teacher who, if I add up all the little segments of time, I think we spent the entire first semester in his vocal pauses. It took him forever to complete a sentence. I wanted to throw things, like SPIT IT OUT!

The only reason for school to be held is the social aspect, because you learn so much about yourself and how to interact with other people. But if school was computer based and you did the lessons on your own time, and you had to go through and teach yourself, it would be so much more useful. I've had incompetent teachers who couldn't teach and when I asked them questions they got mad. I've had teachers who I've completely outsmarted and outwit and I had to wait for them to figure it out. And I'm like "Why am I waiting on an idiot?"

You see kids who think they're smarter than everyone else, and I'd like to think I'm not one of those kids. I try to see things from every angle. Teachers have to deal with a lot of crap too. They have to deal with a lot of kids who don't give them enough credit. They have to deal with a lot of people who aren't giving them any slack. But the worst is when they're just not "there" like when they have no common sense and their administration of their class is in shambles. And they just can't deal with anything. That's when I just want to slam my desk and scream, "Why am I being taught by a dumbass?!"

GK is a 17 year old guy

What would you change about school?

JH: Less intense PE. My PE teacher makes us do all this stuff and my legs are sore after that. I don't really like PE in school. I know that without PE, a lot of people would just sit on the couch all day, but it just doesn't seem like the right thing to put in school.

SL: I would make longer school hours, and cut off Friday, so we could have three-day weekends. Really, when you think about it, you only have one full day to enjoy the weekend. On Friday you only have the night, then you have Saturday. Then you only have part of Sunday, because you have to get ready for the next week of school. Saturday is the only day when I can actually relax and not worry about anything.

JH is a 14 year old girl
SL is a 14 year old girl

What do you wish was taught at school?

GK: The way to deal with people. In elementary school they taught us how to deal with a bully by asking him to please not hit me, and if he did hit me, to go tell a teacher. If I followed that advice in high school I'd be six feet under. They don't tell you how to deal with people and how sick and twisted and how ruthless and horrible some people can be.

When I was in elementary school, I went to a little charter school where all the kids knew each other and the teachers were all nice. And I got into middle school and I started to realize how horrible people are . . . how some people have no morals and don't care.

GK is a 17 year old guy

What has changed since the adults were in school?

MH: Exposure. Not just to things like drugs and alcohol, but to society as a whole, the way things function, the harsh aspects of reality that fall outside those [school] gates. Whether or not the reality that falls outside those gates has changed over the years, we see it more.

MH is a 17 year old guy

What is your school like?

CL: We go to a continuation school.

Do you like this school?

CL: Yes. It's way better than regular school. It's helped us a lot.

What's different here?

CL: We work at our own pace.

AR: And it's less confrontational.

CL: We get to work at our own pace and we get to go to whoever we need at that time instead of being stuck in a big class. Honestly, I used to be a bad kid but this school changed me. It's only 80 kids. And there's less drama and less confrontation.

Confrontation with whom?

AR: With students, with teachers, with faculty, with security, with . . . everybody. I used to get into more confrontations than I did work. But that doesn't happen here.

CL is a 16 year old girl
AR is a 17 year old girl

Who is the person in your family who understands you best?

PO: No one. Well, my mom, she understands me, but she's just so sensitive. She says, "Oh, you had me so worried. You should have called." And I say, "Mom, you shouldn't worry. I can handle myself."

My sisters all went to college. I have three sisters. I'm the black sheep. I don't feel like an outcast or anything. It's just that what I've gone through and what I've done is just totally different from them. One of them was a cheerleader. The other one was a bookworm. The other one was kind of involved in what I was involved in, but she was mostly in crews. I was involved in gangs. And she wasn't really THAT into it. And back then my parents were stricter. Like you have to do what they say and if you ditch you get an ass beating. But with me they were cooler.

I started ditching when I was in elementary school. They didn't find out until I was in middle school. I would literally miss two months. I would just pretend to go and I'd leave early in the morning, and I'd just go somewhere else.

Where would you go?

PO: To my friend's house.

How did your parents find out?

PO: I remember this one time, stupid me, I left my folder in the garage. I don't know how my dad found it, but he saw my folder and he went to school to give it to me and that's when they told him I hadn't been there for a couple of months and he said "What do you mean!? She's been going every day to school." So he got mad and he went to my friend's house, and I was there. I hid.

Didn't the school call to say you were missing?

PO: They called, but I would disconnect the phone, or I would turn the ringer off. And my dad, he's not the brightest. I remember one time I ditched and my best friend and I, we stayed in my room,

Continued . . .

and he would never go in my room. And we were just quiet. We even ordered pizza and he didn't even notice.

So you weren't enjoying school.

PO: No, actually I did enjoy it.

Then why were you ditching?

PO: Because I had better things to do. But I did enjoy it, and I did the work, and I had pretty good grades. The only thing that messed me up was not going. But when I'd go I'd do really good. That's how I passed my classes; we made a compromise. They said, "OK, whenever you come, you better pass all your work." And I did. I really didn't have to go that much.

Have you had any really good teachers?

PO: Yeah, some of them really helped me out. But some of them you could tell they didn't like their job so they didn't really care.

PO is an 18 year old girl

If you could restructure the school experience, what would it look like?

SG: I'd throw a giant rave in the Greek!

Ok . . . I think the way California has it set up, where we have the A through G standards, it makes it so that a lot of classes that kids take they don't like. There are certain private schools that try to offer a wider variety of classes.

This year, now that we are seniors, most of us have enough credits to graduate, so we can pick and choose what we want to take. This year especially I like all my classes and I'm motivated to do my work because I get to choose what I do.

Continued . . .

Early on in high school you are forced to take all these graduation requirements and they suck and it makes people really resent school. So if there is one thing I would change, I'd restructure those things and get rid of classes that there's no long term benefit for.

SG is an 18 year old guy

Tell me about going back to school.

CM: First of all, I'm not a morning person at all. I would wake up, and even though I was up and I was moving, I would stand in the shower for, I swear, ten minutes and let the water hit me and try to let it wake me up. And if someone tried to talk to me I'd be just "uuuuuuuuuuuuhhhh?"

So I was always late for first period. Then if I was late for first period, I didn't even want to go the rest of first period. So I started falling behind in first period. Then I didn't want to go to second period. I just got caught up in ditching. I never really liked school. By the time I got so caught up in ditching, I was so behind in everything that I just stopped going.

The charter school that I'm in now -- I only go two days a week. I feel like I can accomplish more with my life. Me and my friend -- who's in the same situation and goes to the same school as me -- we both feel like we've matured so much more since we've been out of [traditional] school.

I had to qualify for this program. A lot of people are trying to get into this school, but it's only for people like me who were not going to classes at all. Other kids who are still going to classes, it's hard for them to get into this charter school. But because I was losing my school money because I just wasn't going, they let me in.

I was out of school for so long, and now that I'm back on track I feel more accomplished.

CM is a 17-year-old girl

What would you change about school?

MH: I would put more elective choices in our school.

How many electives do you get now?

MH: We only get one a year, unless you do "The Wheel." On the wheel you get a new elective every ten weeks. It's so you can sample the different classes.

SL: The wheel I'm on is computers, art, teen living and then arts and crafts. That makes no sense. I have art twice. I think that we should be able to pick which classes we want on the wheel.

MH: Yes! That would be so much better! Right now there's only language, drafting, band and office practice. They took away yearbook; they took away TA [teacher's assistant].

Why did they take them away?

SL: Because we don't have any money.

MH: My elective class is beginning guitar AND piano, so one teacher has to teach two instruments at the same time.

How many people are in that class?

MH: Forty-one. It's really hard. He gives the pianos a piece of music and sends them to practice while he tunes the guitars and the guitars don't get any time to practice and then we all try to play together and it just doesn't work.

CM: I have office practice.

SL: She has a good elective!

What is office practice?

Continued . . .

CM: It's like where the teachers give you notes and you take them to the different classrooms, like if a student has to go home early or the principal needs to talk to them.

Are you learning anything?

CM: No. We just help out the office people.

MH: Kind of like free labor for the school.

SL: Exactly. Yearbook is an after school activity now, rather than an actual class, and it's not working out. We haven't even started layouts. It's so frustrating. I want yearbook to be a regular class but we can't afford it. All of the electives that I wanted to take aren't there anymore. It's maddening because it's my last year of middle school, we have a new principal, and all these changes are being made.

When you get angry about the budget cuts, what do you do? Do you talk to anyone? Do you have fundraising ideas?

SL: No.
CM: No.

MH is a 15 year old girl
SL is a 14 year old girl
CM is a 14 year old girl

What would you change about school?

NI: Most schools are not created around the idea that school should be a fun place for people to be. But rather, it's just a building for holding people. It's just a building. It has no heart to it. It feels very cold, almost like you're in a hospital.

On top of that, there's a serious lack of communication between students and teachers.

Continued . . .

I feel that kids should be more able to choose their classes and I think that more focus should go into specifically what the kid thinks they want to do for a living. Of course there will always be a need for general education classes, like science and math, but I feel there should be more classes based on religions and world cultures. I feel that, especially here in America, people are not as well educated about the rest of the world as we should be.

I think we need more one-on-one time with our teachers. There needs to be more teachers. And we need to recognize that teachers are really important, and they need to be paid. Hell, we've got baseball payers who are making millions of dollars to play a game for our entertainment. There's got to be a way to move some of that money to the teachers' side of the table. Teachers play such an important part in the world as a whole, because they are essentially bringing up the next generation of human beings.

NI is a 19-year-old guy

Politics

Despite what a politician might stand for,
politics is a game, and there's a way to win.
I find it quite disturbing.

TB is a 17 year old guy

Where do you stand on the political spectrum?

GO: I think of my self as a liberal. But I also kind of think that I'm pretty naive in my thinking. I don't think government does very much for us in terms of our happiness. Government is in place to kind of keep order in things, and I understand why that's necessary in the context of the huge society we have. But on a personal level, I feel that happiness is an internal state that can be reached at any time. And government does not do much for us in that regard, and it's not necessary.

What issues would you like our government to focus on?

GO: One of the big issues for me, that I think is the issue for all other issues, is population control. I know that sounds weird. But China has already addressed that. They limit the number of kids you can have. Almost every problem we have in this society leads back to [the idea that] we have too many people. And it would be nice to see even tiny steps, to see us start to address population control.

GO is an 18 year old guy

What do you see coming up in the next decade?

BT: I don't know. I'm really not that informed on what is coming up.

What do you hope might be coming up?

BT: Well, I can hope that we gradually decrease our dependence on oil. And that we can start putting in legislation to preserve our natural resources and our environment. I don't know if that's going to happen, but I'd like that to happen.

BT is a 17 year old guy

Do you trust our election system?

GK: No! The popular vote means nothing. The Electoral College defeats the entire purpose of democracy. It's why even if I could vote, I probably wouldn't.

What would happen if we abolished the Electoral College and went to a purely one-person-one-vote system?

GK: I think it would be flawed as well. The elections are more about popularity and pointing your finger. They do talk about the issues, but they don't lay it out as clearly as they need to. Instead, they go for cheap shots.

GK is a 17 year old guy

Where do you stand on the political spectrum?

SG: Pretty liberal, but over the recent years, its kind of shifted. My parents are very liberal so of course I was brought up that way. Now that I can vote, I research the issues myself and have different viewpoints. I am pro-gun so that's more to the right. I do believe in individual choice regarding abortion. So I guess that's pro-choice.

I don't like to say I'm republican because that is such a bad party name. But on the more conservative side you are [more about] protecting the rights of the individual. Less government is nice. However, it's hard especially in these times because we're forced to have more government involvement because individuals have proven, just from this economic crisis, they can't make smart decisions on their own. The government sort of has to step in. And that way people fear that the more the government steps into stuff like business and the economy in general, the more they're going to seep into the rest of our lives.

SG is an 18 year old guy

What issues are important to you?

GO: Well, healthcare and education are the two biggest things for me . . . and religion. Healthcare is very hard. People say "Why can't there be universal healthcare?" It's a very fragile subject and it's a very difficult process. There would be major shifting in the government budget. And regarding education, it kind of seems unfair especially when you see the pie charts, how much the military is spending on stuff. But for whatever reason, it doesn't work that way.

But more than money, I think the education system needs to be reformatted. Especially now, because we are falling behind in so many subjects worldwide. Science and math, we are losing all the good scientists. Even if there are good scientists in America, often they will go to Switzerland or Europe because there is less red tape regarding experiments. Additionally less and less people are going towards the medical field. There has got to be a way to attract more people [to these professions].

I'm actually interested in medicine and that's a long road ahead of me. I'm dedicated but it's such a difficult path to walk down. Some people are turned off because it's another 10 years of schooling. People are being deferred to simple business jobs.

Religion is a huge issue for me, like the whole thing of separation of church and state. They say that, but it's weird that in [the last presidency] we had a president who believed it was manifest destiny going into Iraq. So many political agendas are based on religious platforms, like anti-gay marriage and anti-abortion. People think these ways because of their religion. If someone is making decisions for me and my country based on their personal religious point of view, it's not a good thing.

GO is an 18 year old guy

Do you trust our election system?

KS: Not really. It's weird how we elect somebody to go vote for us. It's kind of like we're not really voting. Because even if 90 percent of the votes were for one person, if they don't want that person, it's still up to them. I don't like that. To be honest, I don't understand why we do that. I don't know why they don't just count up the votes.

KS is a 15 year old girl

Where do you stand on the political spectrum?

NI: Do you mean which party do I place my allegiance with? The bipartisan system is very out of date. It's really hard to lump everyone in the United States into two categories.

Protecting the environment, improving education . . these are all things that are talked about, but most of the conversations are about what has happened in the past, and there's a lot of time wasted nitpicking between people like "Oh, he did this." and "She did that and that was bad." But very little energy is focused on what's going to be done.

NI is a 19 year old guy

The Future

I'm just hoping that everyone doesn't blow each other up.

NI is a 19-year-old guy

What's gong to happen after you graduate?

GA: In the summer, hopefully I start going to [a community college]. I am going to study to be a teacher.

GA is a 17-year-old girl

What are you going to do after you graduate?

BT: I want to become a marine biologist, because I love sea animals. I want to be successful at that, and get a degree in that.

I have a lot of goals. Traveling goals, where I want to be when I'm older. But to get to those goals, I would love to be a film producer. I would love to make movies. I'm already working on my own little script thing on my laptop. I love it. I like writing the drama. I haven't worked on it recently though, because eighth grade is such a drag with so much homework. I can never get anything done.

JM: You should join [that school's film club] next year. You can actually make your scripts into reality. And then there are film festivals at school. We just had one. It was where the seniors made movies.

I want to go to college and get a degree for something that gives me enough freedom and enough money because I don't want to struggle with money when I get older. Even if I make a lot of money, I don't want to sit in some boring job and do the same thing everyday. My parents have to struggle with money even though they like what they do. I have a lot of stuff I want to do.

BT is a 17 year old guy
JM is a 16 year old guy

Is the military an option for you?

SG: My brother's good friend has been a Navy Seal for about two years. My family's point of view was that anyone who would go into the military must be some hick who has nowhere to go in life. But seeing him go in was great. He was a straight A student, captain of his water polo team. He got a bunch of scholarships, but he turned them down to enlist. It was good to see someone smart. He's going back to college now.

SG is an 18 year old guy

What is your after school plan?

BB: I want to go to a four-year university. I want to live in New York or San Francisco or LA. I don't know what I want to study because I've gone through a lot of phases where I thought I knew exactly what I wanted to do. But now I don't really. All I know is I really want to go to college. And I really want everything to work out, because the future scares me.

BB is a 16 year old girl

What are you going to do after you graduate?

SP: College. I'm going to study cosmetology and pediatrics.

One of those is medical school.

SP: Yeah, I know. That's why I'm going to try cosmetology first.

SP is a 14-year-old girl

What is going to happen after you graduate?

TB: Oh man, that's the question of the century isn't it? There are an infinite number of possibilities, and I'm looking at all of them and I'm totally scared of all of them. I have the option to go to college to pursue a number of different careers, but in an ideal world I'd like to travel.

With what money?

TB: Exactly. I've come to believe that things don't matter, money doesn't matter, as long as you've got your mind and your body you can go to the places you want to be -- be it a place geographically, like someplace halfway across the world or be it someplace different in the place that you already are. That's what I've been doing for the last few years. I'm constantly re-arranging the position of the place that I'm already in.

TB is a 17 year old guy

What is your big hope for the future?

AA: I have three big dreams that I haven't really decided on. I either want to do something really exciting with an adrenaline rush like a NASCAR driver, or someone who helps other people in different countries. Or a filmmaker. Or I want to open a Mexican restaurant in someplace where Mexican restaurants aren't really there, like France.

AA is a 15 year old girl

What's gong to happen after you graduate?

NZ: Not sure. I want to travel a bit for the summer. That's one of my major plans.

NZ is a 17-year-old girl

What's going to happen after you graduate?

SE: I want to be a photographer. I'm probably going to go to art school and move to San Francisco.

RD: You're so lucky. I want to be a photographer.

What is your photography like?

SE: I usually take pictures of nature, flowers . . . and rain.

RD: Yeah, she likes raindrops. I want to be a photographer as well. I'll probably move to Tokyo. I really like the Japanese culture. It's fascinating to me.

Will you move right after you graduate?

RD: I want to, but it's kind of hard. I have to get the money for it.

SE is a 15 year old girl
RD is a 15 year old girl

What are you going to be when you grow up?

CC: I'm going to be a doctor.

What kind of doctor?

MM: He's going to be a boob surgeon!

ZR: No! Shut up! I want to help people.

Would you be a pediatrician? A veterinarian? A therapist?

ZR: A medical doctor.

ZR is a 14 year old guy
MM is a 15 year old girl

What's coming up in the next 20 years?

TB: Who knows? It's hard to predict anything from where we are right now. The Internet has created subcultures of subcultures of subcultures. It's exploded into a chaos that has never been seen before.

TB is a 17 year old guy

What is your hope for the future?

BT: For me to be healthy.

Is that a challenge?

BT: Sort of.

Why?

BT: I don't want to talk about it.

BT is a 17 year old guy

Ever considered military service?

NI: Yes, many times. Sometimes I still think about it, because I have moments where I doubt my abilities. I really wonder what I'm going to do with myself. I don't know how dependable the people around me are, or what my future holds. The military and the police force are always options for people who are not going to school.

But I remind myself that if I do join the military, I'm far more likely to lose my life and I'll be suffering traumatic situations. It seems to be a very stressful thing. I don't agree with the basis for war. And I don't like killing people.

NI is a 19 year old guy

What are your plans for the future?

KG: I just want to be successful, which I know I will be because I can be a very persuasive, mind-changing person. I can be anything I want to be. I don't let anything hold me back. If I want to do something, I will handle it; I will take care of it. If I stay on this narrow road and don't let side distractions get in my way, I will very, very successful. I do want a college degree. I like writing. Writing is fun. I like poetry.

JC: I want to be a type of businessman. Of what, I'm not sure.

EA: I want one of three careers: Physicist, musician or film director. I want to go to USC, but if I become a physicist, I'm going to Europe.

What can you do in Europe that you can't do here?

EA: A lot more dangerous material, like antimatter. I like weapons. I want to create weapons. And second is musician. I like a lot of heavy metal. And if all else fails, I have dreams that can turn into movies.

KG is a 14 year old girl
JC is a 16 year old guy
EA is a 14 year old guy

What are you going to be when you grow up?

TB: A singer. I'm serious. Don't make fun of me! I'm going to tour with The Jonas Brothers and Justin Bieber. Even if you're not famous, you can still have a good career doing sessions and stuff.

RR: I have, like, 80 options. If I could pick anything, it would be just to have lottery luck.

TB is a 14 year old girl
RR is a 14 year old guy

Do you feel hopeful?

GA: Yeah. I never thought I was going to make it this far.

What do you mean?

GA: I just never thought I'd make it past eighteen.

HM: You thought you were going to get smoked [killed]?

GA: Yeah.

HM: Me too.

GA: Yeah, but now I see myself and I have a son and I graduated and I'm going to go to college and it's like I'm not going to let anything stop me now. And before I didn't care about school or anything. But I want to be a role model for my son. I want to be something in life.

GA is a 17 year old girl
HM is a 19 year old guy

Where are you going to be five years from now?

MM: I'm not sure, but I want to do something with an adrenaline rush. Something fun. Nothing boring. I don't want to hate going to work. I want to actually want to go to work. I'm trying to find ideas.

CC: Hopefully not dead.

HG: All I want is a car.

MM is a 15 year old girl
CC is a 15 year old guy
HG is a 14 year old girl

Do you have a job?

PO: Yeah I'm working. I started working in a [clothing] store. I was the only part-timer that got a raise. Then in January, they made me Assistant.

What would be your ideal job five years from now?

PO: I'd like to be a parole officer.

Have you started looking into what it takes to become a parole officer?

PO: Yeah. I'll have to go to school. I like going to school, but I don't want to waste a bunch of time with [all the prerequisites]. I want to get straight to the point.

PO is an 18 year old girl

What's going to happen when you leave your parents' house?

GO: I'm going to college. I know I'm going to a four-year university, but that's as far as it goes. I can't tell you where I'll be in five years. I can't tell you where I'll be in six months. But I kind of have an idea of what I'd like to be doing.

What if you can't support yourself?

GO: Hopefully that won't be a problem. I am extremely lucky to come from an upper middle class family. My dad has a pretty good job, although money has definitely been an issue recently. And at least one of my parents is willing to support me when I go to school. Of course I'll have to get a part time job and I'll have to support myself in many respects.

And if I can't . . . well, that's not an option.

GO is an 18 year old guy

What do you see coming up in the next decade?

NI: Wow. That's a good question. I'm hoping that media is not going to continue to have such a strangle hold on people. It's almost impossible these days to come out with anything that's unique because it's so quickly publicized and exploited and magnified. The moment you come out with something new, its immediately put on the market, then used, then over used, then laughed at, then scrapped, then picked up and turned into some crappy off take. Ten years from now I'd like to see people generally care about more basic things. Like eating well, loving more.

Media instills this sort of alienating feeling in everyone. It makes people feel that they are the rogue goofball wandering around alone while all the cool kids are having fun together. I'd like there to be more emphasis on humanity as a whole, the idea of everyone living and working together. But I can't really say what I expect to really happen. It's going to be interesting.

NI is a 19-year-old guy

What is going to happen when you graduate and leave your parents house?

GO: I'm going to college, one of the UC's. Hopefully I'll go to Berkeley. Whatever UC I go to, I will be happy with that. I'll do a four-year program with my bachelor's in microbiology or neuro-science, or human behavior. From there, hopefully I will go to med school, and then after 3 years of med school and another year of surgical training I'll begin my residency and then hopefully I'll be a surgeon.

What if you can't make enough to support yourself while you do all this schooling?

GO: If I can't get the loans? My oldest brother is kind of in that

Continued...

pickle right now. My parents have luckily been financially fortunate enough to give him extra cash. If I fell on hard times, my parents could bail me out. It would be a loss of self-respect for me. My biggest fear is being thrown from the nest and not being able to fly. That would suck. I would have to be really down in the dumps before I came crawling back and ask for help.

GO is an 18 year old guy

About Shelly Blaisdell

People talk to me. At bus stops, in the grocery store, in a dentist's waiting room or at the park, some one will sit next to me and start talking. Sometimes hours will pass. They always apologize for taking my time. I always thank them for trusting me, for giving me a glimpse into a life that I never knew existed before that day.

One day on the bus a man told me all about keeping his little sister safe while crossing the border from Mexico. He recalled some of the jokes they told while riding in a dark truck for hours. He missed his stop while we were laughing.

One day at the park a 78 year old woman told me all about learning to be loud and bold as she slowly became invisible to everyone under the age of 50. She also told me the great fun being invisible can be, and how interesting it is to lay down a lifetime of being nice and raising her voice.

One day a houseless woman stopped by my porch asking for socks and before the day was over, she invited me to her home behind an empty building and showed me her drawings. She worked in charcoal because she could find bits of it on the beach.

I consider these events gifts. When someone chooses me to receive what is often a story that's never been told before, I am honored and usually awestruck by what I hear. Of course I am sometimes horrified, but never bored.

But listening takes time. So I decided to make it my career. Now I choose issues that are important and seek storytellers who live those issues. It's truly a charmed existence. I learn amazing things and meet interesting people everyday.

This book, The LA Teen project is the first of many more to come.

I hope this book has opened your eyes to the activities and thoughts of a very large part of our city, our Teens, the ones who live in our neighborhoods, not the ones you see on television.

Thank you for reading!

Shelly Blaisdell

www.ingramcontent.com/pod-product-compliance
Lightning Source LLC
Chambersburg PA
CBHW072045280526
45788CB00006B/2190